Right on the Money

ADVANCE PRAISE FOR
RIGHT ON THE MONEY

Colleen Francis has been an integral transformational sales leader for RelaDyne. As the market leader with ongoing acquisitions, our continual RelaDyne challenge is the professional evolution of our sales force. With Colleen's guidance and expertise, RelaDyne has pivoted to a post-COVID sales organization optimizing technology, value-based selling, account planning, retention, analytics, and advanced coaching techniques. She is valued, honest, and always on point.

Dan Oehler, EVP, RelaDyne

Colleen Francis has taken Orbitform's sales to the next level. With her expertise in sales strategy and tactics, she has expertly coached us through the infamously difficult 2020 selling year and built momentum for an exceptional 2021. We are playing at a higher level because of Colleen Francis. Right on the Money provides a roadmap to all businesses for similar success.

Phil Sponsler, President, Orbitform

I've admired Colleen Francis for two decades for her deep talent in active sales coaching and engagement. Colleen has proven that she is a master of her field, not only due to her vast experience as a sales leader across many industries but also because of the process she brings to meaningful change. It's not enough to just tell others what and how to do – the lessons must be repeated using many mediums, in a dynamic way that resonates with sellers and their leaders. Thank you Colleen for packaging so much of your knowledge in Right on the Money – it's always a good time to sell, now more than ever.

Kathryn Tremblay, CEO, Exel / Altis HR

Colleen Francis "gets it." She doesn't rely on cookie cutter sales techniques from decades ago, she understands what works in today's challenging business-to-business sales environment. Not only did she help our team perform on a new level, her insights for our sales leadership team set us up to continue achieving those results – no matter what challenges we face in the future.

Katy McFee, VP Sales, Evidence Partners

Colleen Francis has been a key part of our team as we transform our sales organization in this competitive, volatile market. Her ability to quickly assess the opportunities has meant accelerated client acquisition and increased share of wallet growth. Colleen's guidance is clear and frank, and the strategies in Right on the Money provide the opportunity for immediate and lasting results.

Steve Moore, CEO, Parman Energy Group

RIGHT ON THE MONEY

New Principles for Bold Growth

COLLEEN FRANCIS

NEW YORK

LONDON • NASHVILLE • MELBOURNE • VANCOUVER

Right on the Money

New Principles for Bold Growth

Published in New York, New York, by Morgan James Publishing. Morgan James is a trademark of Morgan James, LLC. www.MorganJamesPublishing.com

Proudly distributed by Ingram Publisher Services.

A **FREE** ebook edition is available for you
or a friend with the purchase of this print book.

CLEARLY SIGN YOUR NAME ABOVE

Instructions to claim your free ebook edition:
1. Visit MorganJamesBOGO.com
2. Sign your name CLEARLY in the space above
3. Complete the form and submit a photo
   of this entire page
4. You or your friend can download the ebook
   to your preferred device

ISBN 9781631956713 paperback
ISBN 9781631956720 ebook
Library of Congress Control Number:
2021940433

Cover & Interior Design by:
Christopher Kirk
www.GFSstudio.com

Morgan James is a proud partner of Habitat for Humanity Peninsula
and Greater Williamsburg. Partners in building since 2006.

Get involved today! Visit MorganJamesPublishing.com/giving-back

*To all the sellers who worked tirelessly in both challenging
times to keep their customers and their businesses buoyant.
I am inspired by your stories, your success, and your ability to
consistently leverage the changes that were thrown at you daily.*

TABLE OF CONTENTS

ACKNOWLEDGMENTS

While every client I have worked with deserves to be acknowledged for their contributions to this book, there are five in particular without whom this book would not be.

Thank you to the customers who shared their success personally for the examples in this book. Your generous spirit of partnership will help many sellers and businesses improve dramatically

To the incredibly patient team at Morgan James who bared with me when I realized in April of 2020 that the entire manuscript had to be rewritten, as our world as sellers was completely upside down.

Thank you to my editors and designers Patrick Gant and Brian O'Mera-Croft. Your thoughtful commentary and professional guidance resulted in a book that moves the discussion of selling to a new level of sophistication.

A debt of gratitude to my long-standing Director of Operations Casey Forster. Your loyalty to Engage and support of our clients continue to allow me to simultaneously write this book while continuing to do what I love to do best, work with our clients.

Finally, thank you to my husband and business partner Chris. Your unwavering support and inspiration motivates all my work.

INTRODUCTION

Even before COVID-19 upended the lives of nearly every person on Earth—and forced us to reimagine our every interaction with others—the notion of "business as usual" tottered unsteadily on its last legs. The coronavirus simply roared in and ran it over.

For years we felt technology and innovation quake the fragile ground beneath our tradition-loving feet. In less than a generation, we moved from feeding quarters into pay phones at malls and airports to carrying sophisticated tools for computing, photography, music, film, communication, and more in a single handheld device. After decades of newspapers, radio, television, and cable dominating information and entertainment, we flocked to online streaming, always-on social media, and near-instant access to the world's accumulated knowledge (and misinformation).

An overwhelmingly digital economy liberated us from an archaic bricks-and-mortar mindset and gave rise to a brave new mobile world. We no longer need a physical office to do business, nor must we live close to our customer. All we need to set up shop—and to emerge as a fierce competitor—is a mobile device, an internet connection, and a hunger for success. Remember the old AT&T jingle "Reach out and touch someone"? Today's mantra might instead be "Click. Connect. Buy."

Just a handful of years moved us from identifying and wooing customers based on informed hunches to swimming in a vast ocean of increasingly granular market data, much of which fuel machine-learning technologies certain to elevate targeting to whole new levels.

Top sellers took notice—and took heed—as tried-and-true methods of selling, marketing, and working with others gradually lost their punch. They began to evolve, to modify plans and behaviors to better navigate an oft-shifting landscape.

Others, alas, stuck to their guns and wasted precious time yearning for how things once were. They complained about the difficulty and impersonal nature of online meetings. They mourned the loss of face-to-face contact, of the reassuring handshake that sealed a deal. They feared and thus gave a wide berth to new technology. Messages about the need to adapt fell on deaf ears. As we clamor today to uncover any silver lining amid the global pandemic and ensuing economic shutdown, consider this: for better or worse, we're *all* finally getting the message.

Here's a big, scary fact you may not like to hear—but that you must accept:

Nobody *sells* anymore. We've moved from a *sell-to* model to a *buy-from* environment. People buy on their own terms now—and often without salespeople!

Refusing to adapt to a changing world condemned many salespeople to failure. Sadly, the same proved true for long-standing institutions. Why didn't Sears morph into what Amazon is today? Maybe they overlooked or ignored emerging risks. Perhaps they proved too big, bulky, and unyielding to swiftly change course. Individuals and organizations alike kept blinders on while the world morphed around them.

Thanks in part to the pandemic, most of us shop online a lot more often, even for very large purchases. Self-service is on the rise in all industries, and buyers today prefer the simplicity, convenience, and anonymity of remote interactions. I count myself among this group. Recently I self-configured my new car purchase from my phone; I selected the make, model, and features; sent my wishes to the dealer; and placed an order without ever setting foot in a showroom.

Today we sellers feel frustrated and lost because we no longer steer the sales bus; when we least expected it, the customer snatched the wheel. We no longer serve as buyers' primary source of information; in fact, customers move through much of the buying cycle before ever engaging sellers—if they invite us in at all. If you feel cut out of the process—marginalized and lacking control—you have every right. Still, to stay in the game, you must cease clamoring for the world to fall back into how you define "normal." Clinging to lost history drives buyers away from your sales team and sends profits out of your business.

In years past sellers served as the go-to source for information about products or services. No more. Today buyers track down their own subject matter experts: peers, their own networks and communities, even reviews and testimonials they uncover from basic web searches. These buyers count heavily on consensus and thus seek out and engage a surprisingly large chorus of voices in making buying decisions. This creates a longer, more complex sales cycle.

Buyers today base decisions more on data than on personal relationships with sellers. Armed with their own research and connections, they answer your calls only when they feel certain you offer them something new and valuable—something *extra.* And when they do deign to work with a personal seller, their top priority is customer centricity: in other words, they expect you to tailor the entire process to them and their needs.

For reasons that evade me, I feel surprised when sellers share this same thinking when making their own personal purchases and yet somehow convince themselves the B2B universe plays by a wholly different set of rules. Nope. Consider just how easily our consumer buying habits carry over into business:

A while back I needed new office equipment. Over the years a local AV company just miles from my office had provided for such needs, so I called to make a purchase. They didn't have my desired item in stock, so I asked them to order it. I then learned they wouldn't take the order over the phone, nor would they allow me to pay with a credit card. Annoyed, I let them know I would neither agree to a face-to-face visit nor reward them with my business. Instead, I searched for options online, ordered from a company thousands of miles away, and enjoyed my new purchase inside a week. Because this AV company refused to evolve—and behaved in anything but a customer-centric fashion—they lost my patronage forever.

Losing one small sale may seem like no big deal—after all, a single item stings much less than hundreds of thousands of dollars or more, so what possible influence might my piddling three hundred bucks have on larger, complex sales? Think about my habits. Because I no longer offer my business to that store, it is, to me, essentially obsolete—I no longer buy there, nor will I recommend it to others. My online vendor gets my business and any referrals. I now trust this system, with its reviews, options, and clear delivery timelines, more than any brick-and-mortar alternative. What's more, trust is scalable. I can now easily think, "If this worked out for a three-hundred-dollar purchase, why wouldn't it work equally well for an item costing $3,000?" Before long I find myself applying the same philosophy to one-hundred-thousand-dollar products.

Those paying attention saw abundant warning signs long before 2020 hit like a category four hurricane. And yet some foolish optimists still imagine customers may host in-person meetings rather than embrace videoconferencing as the standard. Others wait on the sales floor for the customer to come to them. Still others double down on cold calling, as though it may suddenly turn into sales more than 0.3 percent of the time.[1] Remarkably, more than a few still rely on direct mail and print ads, as though trapped forever in 1982. These dinosaurs wait for the customers to come. They wait. And they wait. And as they wait, their win rates stagnate; after all, closing ratios have held steady at around 29 percent since the 1980s!

---

1   Steven MacDonald, "38 Social Selling Statistics: How to Master the Art of Social Selling," *SuperOffice*, March 14, 2019, https://www.superoffice.com/blog/social-selling-statistics/.

The bottom line is this: accept and embrace change, or you're done in sales. Just as Amazon and Shopify are the new "department stores," you, the traditional salesperson, can easily be replaced.

Take a breath. I've beaten you down with bad news. Now get ready for something encouraging. You *can* capitalize on the new selling landscape. In fact, you can take hold of the opportunity of a lifetime. You can broaden your reach *and* your bottom line, all while becoming more efficient. All the top-ranked sales leaders with whom I work know this. They quietly made changes and kept their new thinking and updated practices to themselves, all while racking up massive wins.

I'm here to share what worked for them so you can win too. But you must be ready to change both your mindset and how you work as a seller or leader of sellers. You must redesign processes. You must open your eyes to recognize and harness changes in the sales landscape. You must shed outdated notions in favor of adaptation and growth.

You hold in your hands an essential handbook to understand and win over today's buyers. Join me as I shed light on the current sales landscape, how it reflects buyers' interests and demands, and how you can align both your personal and organizational strategies to win. I offer a wealth of field-tested, actionable steps to achieve accelerated growth results. I better prepare you to excel in a marketplace that is far more digital, far less centralized, more incredibly dynamic, and, yes, much more lucrative than ever before.

I also share cautionary tales of those who are failing to change—those too busy closing new deals to notice such a need. If you live in this camp, this book offers a vital wake-up call. You must apply a whole new set of skills and assumptions to succeed and to achieve the growth you expect for your organization—and that your organization most definitely expects from you.

Whether you're an ambitious seller, a team leader, or a senior executive, you'll find in this book a proven, realistic game plan to redraw the maps of how you think about sales and marketing in a topsy-turvy world. When we finish, you, your team, and your organization will all be Right on the Money.

Chapter 1

THE LANDSCAPE
HAS CHANGED

*We're in a new digital world ... The past is gone and it's
not coming back ... We need to rebuild our companies,
our organizations and ultimately, we need
to rebuild ourselves to be successful.*
—Marc Benioff, CEO, Salesforce, September 23, 2020

Writer Gordon Livingston, MD, once penned, "If the map doesn't agree with the ground, the map is wrong." If you work in sales and marketing today—either as a seller or as a leader of sellers—and you have yet to overhaul rules governing how you connect with customers, *your* map is wrong. **The sales landscape has changed because everything else has.**

- As of 2020 more than half the world—or 4.7 billion people—is now online. Most connect via mobile devices.
- More than $80 trillion (USD) makes up the world economy.
- The average person today is more than four times richer than in 1950.
- By 2020 e-commerce constituted 16 percent of all retail sales, and it should grow to 22 percent by 2023 (or perhaps sooner because of global events in 2020).
- A World Economic Forum report notes that following the onset of COVID-19, internet use jumped more than 70 percent, use of communication apps doubled, and some video streaming services saw daily use rise twentyfold. "Never have we been so aware of our dependence on digital models," they conclude. "And we are not going back."

"The LinkedIn State of Sales Report 2020" zeroes in on even more immediate trends for today's sales managers, some of which specifically relate to the global pandemic and resulting business lockdowns:

- 77 percent hold more virtual meetings;
- 44 percent expect a decrease in responsiveness to outreach efforts;
- 44 percent anticipate a longer sales cycle; and
- 70 percent agree a manager's capacity to navigate change is more important today than five years ago.

"More than ever," the report argues, "transformation is an inescapable reality in the sales organization, and the pace of change is only accelerating."

This reality is echoed by an insightful Gartner in their Future of Sales 2025 report that imagines what sales will look like into the next decade: "By 2025, sales organizations will require sellers to develop new digital skills, using digital channels for remote selling or co-selling to customers." What's more, "Sellers' decision making will be based on data, analytics and AI, not on intuition and experience."

And yet, even while facing this mountain of evidence, many sellers and business leaders *still pretend nothing has changed!*

In just a single week this year, I fell slack jawed as I witnessed a half dozen outdated sales techniques and wrongheaded ways to handle customers:

- I received a cold email chirping, "You requested information to better your dental practice," when, clearly, I had not.
- I saw high-value, sales-ready leads withering to stagnation in a customer relationship management (CRM) system;
- I watched as a lack of account planning led to a full-on mutiny, with zero warning, by half of one team's customers to an RFP;
- I talked with financial sellers who, while trying to build rapport with a prospect through a series of questions, heard: "I gave that information to your inside salesperson last week";

- I heard sales leaders refusing to coach top performers because "I don't want to babysit"; and
- I saw sellers organizing sales calls based on the day of the week and alphabetically.

Such madness must stop—right now.

Early in 2020, rapidly evolving technologies collided with quick-developing events, and as a result—and like it or not—everything and everyone changed. Others can debate the causes; as a sales coach who has studied habits of top-ranked sellers for more than two decades, I'm most interested in the effect of these changes. Plainly stated: **market and sales power now rest in the hands of the buyer.**

Many companies responded to this shift by investing heavily in solutions that reward sales departments with a never-before-seen bounty: detailed insights into buyer behavior, high-quality leads, and a window into quick-changing market trends. In essence, technology bestows superpowers to sellers—and yet far too many squander these advantages. They pair this powerful punch with a flaccid, timeworn sales strategy. They manage prospects and interact with buyers in ways certain to fall short: they *sell to* customers rather than luring customers to *buy from* them.

The facts speak for themselves: closing ratios have barely budged much past 31 percent … in forty years! One client with a highly established and well-equipped marketing department owned up to a closing rate of just 13 percent. Ineffective methods like cold-calling clung to life far beyond their best-before dates, despite solid research revealing they turn into sales only

0.3 percent of the time.[2] Today buyers move through much of the sales cycle on their own. Technology and innovation—including machine-learning, artificial-intelligence-enhanced interactions—help sellers easily create their own high-value customer experience.

So where is the disconnect?

Key sales metrics have yet to improve because sales leaders insist on telling themselves the old way of doing things is "just how selling is done," when they should recognize a clear and troubling problem in need of fixing. Still, something even deeper is going on. Some sellers, upon hearing that customers keep cutting salespeople out of the buying process, wrongly accept that this foretells the inevitable end of salespeople. Not true—this represents an evolutionary moment for sales, not an extinction event! Those who survive will have seen and understood the distinction between the landscape and the map in this new sales environment.

This Is a B2All World Now

Selling strategies for B2B (business to business) were once very different from those for B2C (business to consumer). The former employed a rapport-heavy, fact-driven, risk-averse approach that kept sellers in control; the latter thrived in a climate fueled by impulse, emotion, and buyers' interests and timelines. Our new landscape comes with a new set of rules that obliterate **lines between B2B and B2C selling strategies. Buyers—not sellers—now hold control.**

---

2   Steven MacDonald, "38 Social Selling Statistics," *SuperOffice* (blog), January 14, 2021, https://www.superoffice.com/blog/social-selling-statistics/.

Buyers today expect much the same experience ordering costly industrial equipment for their factory as they do dropping a few dollars on jeans for their children. They employ the same processes to inform buying decisions. They expect ease of access, better selection, and instant gratification—reinforced by bulletproof payment and delivery options, along with solid recommendations from other buyers. This *Amazonification* of sales is reshaping all aspects of every selling environment.

In other words: **B2B and B2C have simply become B2All.**

Thriving companies and sellers understand this shift. They know we no longer live in a *sell-to* marketplace; we exist in a *buy-from* marketplace. They understand generating revenue reliably means focusing both on *external expectations of customers* and *internal business processes* to create ideal buying conditions.

The key to succeeding in sales today is to become Right on the Money, where you combine a customer-centric revenue model with new improvements to your Sales Velocity that put the buyer and their unique needs in the front seat.

Changes have created a dichotomy where it's both easier and more difficult for sellers to succeed. With an abundance of tools and information now available, we can reach more people, using more channels, and much faster than ever before. These same circumstances also complicate things, because in an environment crowded with options and content, we must do much more to make our mark and capture business. Do things right and you uncover a wealth of opportunities; get the process wrong and you risk damaging your position in the marketplace.

The Future of Sales: A Formula for Success

For companies to be Right on the Money, they must navigate a new map—and adopt a fresh sales strategy. They must balance a customer-centric outlook, externally focused on customer demands, with the need to create improvements in Sales Velocity (an internal focus on sales processes). A bell curve with *customer centricity* on the left and *Sales Velocity* on the right captures this balance; those who focus evenly on factors within and outside their organizations thrive, while those that lean too much toward one end or the other cause an imbalance sure to result in far less desirable outcomes.

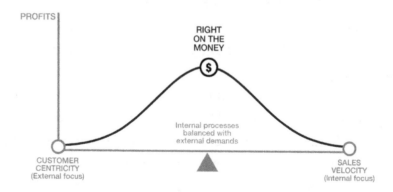

Companies at the far right of the scale focus too heavily on Sales Velocity without accounting for customer centricity. These businesses "sell at all costs." Remember the overenthusiastic sales team at Wells Fargo that not long ago garnered plenty of unflattering headlines for their overbearing and beyond-questionable sales practices? Meanwhile, companies at the far left dote on customers at the expense of all other business requirements: they sell at a loss, accept poor terms, offer too much choice, and generally confuse customers into not buying. Retailers like Sears, Macy's, and JCPenney felt certain they were still doing right by the customer, only to realize—too late—not all customer-centric processes translate into profitable business practices. These businesses needed strategies to improve Sales Velocity; they never got there, and now they're on the ropes or gone altogether.

Companies that strike an ideal balance include the typical darlings of business—Apple and Southwest Airlines, for starters—along with thousands of forward-thinking business-to-business companies. Both small and large, they present the strongest evidence a business can successfully adapt to a changed marketplace, as we'll explore in upcoming chapters.

Adopting a balanced strategy is nonnegotiable. Take a lead from Amazon CEO Jeff Bezos, who says: "Your margin is my opportunity."[3] You may not yet be in direct competition with Amazon, but you almost certainly compete with someone willing to offer a lower price. The "lowest price provider" exists in every business and consumer market worldwide. Your only way to win is by both staying customer-focused and making your sales processes fast and profitable, with increased velocity through customer centricity.

How This Book Is Organized

This book comprises two parts. In the first, I showcase four core realities reshaping today's sales landscape and reveal how you can best enhance customer centricity:

---

3   Matt Turner, "One of Jeff Bezos' Most Famous Quotes is a Warning to Wall Street," *Business Insider*, March 5, 2018, https://www.businessinsider.com/one-of-jeff-bezos-most-famous-quotes-is-a-warning-to-wall-street-2018-3.

1. **Your brand is your time**—Understand what you must change to make it easy for people to do business with you.

2. **You must take ownership of your story**—You define your character in the story being told about you, online and elsewhere.

3. **Critical mass influence**—You must understand and leverage the importance of the people modifier.

4. **Be broad where others are narrow**—You must harness the power of a marketplace that features multiple discrete perspectives.

Once we consider how each factor affects the present and future of selling, we move to the second half of *Right on the Money*: how to skillfully balance customer centricity and Sales Velocity.

1. **Sales Velocity**—Understand and measure how fast you and your team make sales and earn revenue.

2. **Corporate velocity**—Bring a changed mindset about sales and revenue into your organization.

3. **Be smart about working with data**—Learn to select and control your sales data so they yield meaningful, measurable results.

4. **Coaching culture**—Build and grow a coaching framework and make it part of your personal career development plan.

Achieving balance makes you Right on the Money. Let's start on our journey to learn how this is done.

Chapter 2

TIME-BASED BRANDING

Do you ever find yourself immersed in a compelling, rapid-fire text exchange—volleying ideas, attitudes, and LOLs back and forth—only to groan or scream when the conversation grinds to an inexplicable, screeching halt? We all do. The speed of communication today renders us all brutally impatient and makes time an ultra-premium commodity.

To be Right on the Money today, sales organizations must recognize *time* has become a vital new brand—people have so little to spare, and they fully control how, when, and where they spend it.

We find ourselves flooded daily with information. As consumers we delve into our own research rather than entrust this step to sellers, who might lead us astray or otherwise waste our time. We demand sellers stand at the ready in case we may need them and expect a near-instant response. We bring our business to organizations who embrace a new paradigm: time-based branding.

To thrive (or at least survive), your organization must make it simple for people to do business with you. You must save buyers' time while reinforcing their confidence and trust. In doing so you create a frictionless buying experience, one to which buyers will flock again and again. **Think of it as "Amazon-Priming" your business**. Anything you do to take up fewer of those precious minutes helps define you as customer-centric and primes you to win.

By contrast, if you waste your customer's treasured time, expect heaps of hardship ahead. Consider cold-calling: if not completely dead already, the overwhelming move to digital in a post pandemic world stands poised to pound the final nail into its coffin.[4] Our traditional approach to sales—centered around frequent phone calls and face-to-face meetings with customers and potential buyers—also faces certain demise. Buyers say no because they have too much going on.

Time-based branding is crucial, because it saves both you and your buyer time and, in doing so, makes you *and* your buyer more profitable! To take full advantage, you must embrace three key strategies: use speed to anticipate; be a one-stop shop with a variety of relevant products under one roof (or website); and be easy to buy from. Let's examine each element.

---

4   "The Death of Cold Calling—Ending the Debate," *Inside View*, March 18, 2011, https://blog.insideview.com/2011/03/18/the-death-of-cold-calling-ending-the-debate/.

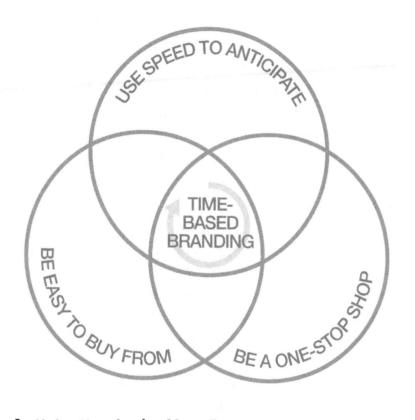

Anticipation Is the New Responsiveness

Back in the day, buyers knew nothing of us—not even of our existence—until we called to make an introduction. Now we have no idea who *they* are until they pop up and demonstrate a readiness to buy. At that point there's zero time to waste. We live in a "wait, wait, wait, hurry up!" reality: as sellers we must use speed to convert prospects into customers.

Speed Wins

Today buyers turn to a select few suppliers—ones prequalified through their own research—and then usually go with the fastest. Our research at Engage Selling shows that the company that responds first comes away with **75 percent of orders**. If you fail to reply within twenty-four hours, kiss any order goodbye. You must never lag behind those competitor's adept at showing up quickly—who often win even with higher prices!

I work with two different companies competing in the same industry. Both enjoy the same number of monthly web-based sales leads generated from the same automated marketing platform—but each achieves different results.

Company A lacks a systematic response process for leads. They allow for up to a forty-eight-hour gap between the time a lead comes in and first contact with the prospect. They convert a measly 1.3 percent of leads to qualified opportunities. They don't measure their closing rate, but even if they closed every opportunity, they would only see 1.3 wins for every 100 leads.

Meanwhile, Company B immediately responds to each new lead using automated-response software built into their marketing platform. The sales team must get back to the customer within an hour. They convert 22 percent of leads to qualified opportunities, of which they close 80 percent. With seventeen new sales, they outperform Company A by more than a twelve-to-one margin!

In short, Company B outperforms Company A primarily because their data shows them to treat speed as a priority. They learned potential buyers were seven times more likely to engage with them if they responded within an hour. This success reveals a key truth: **hot leads stay hot for minutes, not days. Don't sacrifice yours to unnecessary delays.**

Show Up with Power in the Room

Another key to accelerating your sales process is to start off with the right people in the room. Executives make faster decisions than do worker bees tasked with gathering and feeding information slowly up the chain. How do you snare the attention of decision makers? Show up with power. When you inject your own higher-ups into the conversation, you soon discover likeness attracts likeness. Executives also buy quicker when speaking to peers than when facing lower-level sellers.

One client uncovered this missing link after, over and over, they lost business on one important account. This buyer would come to them only for small orders; multimillion-dollar contracts went first to tender and then consistently to my client's competitor. Why? Because each time a request for proposal arrived, the executive team opted against going to the meetings. Without power in the room, the customer felt jilted. Meanwhile, the competitor's top brass would hop on a plane, powwow with the buyer's leaders, and nail down the sale. They shortened the process and thus cemented deals quickly and easily by cultivating conversations between peers and making the buyer feel loved.

Team-selling between manufacturers and distributors improves the number, size, and quality of deals for these reasons:

1. Multiple sets of eyes and ears on the account mean no question stays unasked, which results in a more comprehensive understanding of customer needs.
2. Customers feel encouraged to bring more buyers and influencers to the table, which helps speed up decisions.

3. Buyers feel they receive more attention and resources, which enhances the sales team's image.
4. Sellers learn from each other and employ these new skills to secure new opportunities.

To recap: Timing is everything. You must involve the right people on both sides. Remember this, and you move that much closer to securing a sale *now*. Of course, you must offer what customers want to buy, which brings us to …

Create a One-Stop Shop

Every time your customer chooses to buy, they face both risk and their own perceptions of *how much* risk they face. They ask: "Can I be sure I'm making a good choice? What if things don't work out? What's the cost of failure?"

To hedge bets against lost money and time, buyers tend to stick with sellers with whom they've done business before. Many large businesses embrace such *vendor consolidation*—turning to fewer vendors to meet buying needs—to cut down on extraneous expenses and to minimize risk.

Each time a business creates a purchase order and cuts a check, it eats up additional time and energy as personnel manage the process. Reducing the number of vendors pares down the work and thus the dollars lost. Fewer suppliers also means less risk inherent in ramping up activities and procedures with unfamiliar parties—something with which we all deal when embarking on a new relationship. An existing supplier—one whom buyers know and trust—can offer the wanted simplicity and security.

Vendor consolidation thrives also because it recognizes a shift in the way we buy. Retail companies bucking the downward revenue trend and doing well—even before the lockdowns drove buying online—thrive because they are all one-stop shops offering the convenience consumers now trust and respect.

When grocery giant Loblaw bought drug chain Shoppers Drug Mart in Canada, they immediately moved a small but popular selection of products from one chain onto the shelves of the other. This created upsell opportunities in both and reduced the need for customers to shop elsewhere.

Similarly, Amazon continues to diversify into a dizzying number of industries, including prescriptions, mobile, healthcare, and more. Walmart and Target have now jumped into the game, adding groceries, food kiosks, healthcare services, and high-end products to their initial offerings. These are all customer-centric decisions.

Today business buyers demand the same one-stop convenience—especially as more who have grown up with "buying with one click" enter the workforce. As a client recently told me: "We're either going to sell on Amazon or become the Amazon of the industrial supply business." He understands that to remain competitive, his company has no choice but to offer customers more. Companies failing to get on board soon fall by the wayside.

Consider two B2B examples that illustrate why becoming a one-stop shop is proving so important:

First, a large manufacturing client seemed certain to lose to vendor consolidation a huge contract worth million. The twist? The organization already offered everything the buyer needed—

but their customer had *no idea*. A series of acquisitions meant the business owned six different brands, all of which operated independently with different names and salespeople. This buyer—a multinational consumer goods company—routinely bought from each of my client's brands but never knew they were all part of the same company!

When the buyer approached one brand to inform them of plans to pull their business because it didn't offer four additional products—all of which fell under my client's umbrella—this client quickly realized they needed to operate as a single source. They inked a new deal under a single corporate name and consolidated ordering and payment processes, which reduced the number of sellers calling on the client and improved profitability for both.

Texas-based Arnold Oil Company understands the value of one-stop shopping. They were able to capitalize on product diversity during the 2020 economic downturn. As a supplier of automotive products, shop equipment, lubricants, fuels, and outdoor power equipment, they soon realized that offering such a broad array positioned them to not only weather the storm but rebound faster as the economy recovered. In fact, they own a greater share of the market than they did before the world shut down.

Getting Right on the Money: Quick Tip

Reap the benefits of becoming a one-stop shop for your customers—here's how:

- Decouple product and service bundles to offer more options. For example, many restaurants that survived the pandemic transformed their meal service into grocery items and butcher shops.

- Offer a multistep plan for maintenance, training, and customer service, promoted as "gold, silver, and bronze" levels. While some customers may desire in-person service and training, others may prefer to keep everything virtual for now. Why not offer both?
- If you sell products, add services. Training, consulting, and implementation support are all added-value options. The same goes for service sellers. Uncharted Consulting recently launched their first product after twenty years in business. Within two years, product sales constituted 10 percent of revenue.
- Create reseller or referral relationships with complementary companies.
- Add new products that complement your business and satisfy your market's needs. My client Orbitform attends an annual industry trade show, always with a new product to display. In fact, they've made it a rule: "No new product, no attendance." Since attending the show is profitable, this requirement keeps them listening to customers' needs and creating products to address them. As a result, they consistently win innovation awards and outperform the previous year.

Be Easy to Buy From

Taking two important steps—using speed to anticipate and becoming a one-stop shop—increases your odds of lasting success, but you must do more. You must also make it effortless for people to buy from you. Any snags slow things down, peg you as unfriendly to customers, and seriously damage your ability to sell.

One client sought my help in finding and installing a new customer relationship management (CRM) system. This was a large purchase—about $300,000—so, like most buyers today, we threw ourselves into our research. By the time I contacted the CRM company on my client's behalf, we knew exactly what we wanted. Also like most buyers, we needed the software with sufficient urgency to be keen to cut a check.

Alas, the seller was not yet ready for us. Before I could speak with a sales rep, I needed to fill out a long online form revealing my client's name, size, and the timeframe in which we wanted to buy. A sales rep then called and repeated the very questions I had answered online. After I relayed the information again, he informed me that, based on my client's industry—also clearly stated on the form—he would need to transfer me to an account manager. I waited impatiently for that person to call, only to have the new contact barrage me with the same questions *again*.

Either the sales rep had failed to enter notes into the CRM—ironically, the very system I was trying to buy—or the account manager called before checking the data in front of him. Regardless, the waste of my time caused my frustration to spike.

Undeterred, the account manager asked, "Would you like a thirty-day trial?" My client and I did not; we already knew what we wanted and were ready to buy. Unfortunately, because no one bothered to listen, we took our business elsewhere.

This cautionary tale warns how salespeople and companies can hamstring their own success with complex, redundant buying processes. The good news is we *can* do better. Consider three simple, customer-centric opportunities to improve:

1. Toss out sales development rep (SDR) or cold-calling teams; they only frustrate buyers and strain your recruiting process. Each time you pass a buyer over to a new person, exasperation blooms and trust erodes.

2. Keep your inside sales team, but reorient them 180 degrees to become the most senior team on your sales force. Why leave the toughest and most important job—finding the right buyers for your most valuable products—in the hands of your greenest sellers? Doesn't it seem backward to make senior-level buyers feel you waste their time with people unable to help?

3. Streamline tools and information to ensure everyone enjoys centralized access to all information gathered from the buyer. The best way is to maintain a single portal for customer information and to require everyone to use it. You paid a lot of money for that fancy CRM—shouldn't you expect a return on your investment?

Selling to the Always-On Buyer

As we think about today's buyers—each strapped for time, wary of sellers, and overwhelmingly swayed by peers—keep in mind what may well happen with their younger cohorts. Millennials already outnumber Baby Boomers in the workplace.[5] Members of

---

5   Richard Fry, "Millennials Projected to Overtake Baby Boomers as Largest Generation," Pew Research Center, March 1, 2018, http://www.pewresearch.org/fact-tank/2018/03/01/millennials-overtake-baby-boomers.

Gen Z—today's youngest adults—represent a whopping 25 percent of the US population and will soon overtake everyone else at the water cooler.[6] Perhaps the biggest difference between younger generations and those before is that they've never known a world without ubiquitous computers and mobile devices. As they rise to senior positions, they will doubtless bring ever-evolving technological tools with them. The changes in the market landscape will become more and more evident—and inescapable.

Technology will continue to play an extensive role, with certain elements continuing to evolve as others fade. For example, some organizations are shedding voicemail for employees whose roles aren't customer-facing, thus saving themselves hundreds of thousands of dollars on a tool much less frequently used and valued.

When personal computers entered offices in the 1980s and 1990s, businesses set the standard for the technologies employees used. Now employees often identify and personally acquire the most cutting-edge technology and incorporate it into both their home and work lives—a single-tool, "bring-your-own-device (BYOD)" philosophy organizations could never have imagined just years ago. The blending of personal and work devices has deepened further since 2020, when workers tied to their home began to multitask professional activities, homeschooling, communication, and entertainment.

To better manage stress, employees often tackle low-hanging fruit—simple tasks like researching products and services—

---

6   Kathryn Dill, "7 Things Employers Should Know About the Gen Z Workforce," *Forbes*, November 6, 2015, https://www.forbes.com/sites/ kathryndill/2015/11/06/7-things-employers-should-know-about-the-gen-z- workforce/#631d4db2fad7.

at home and after hours, which further blurs the lines between when people are on and off the clock.[7]

How does this affect sellers? As more of us use our own tech to work from anywhere, the portion of research conducted online—currently 27 percent—will continue to expand, as will online purchasing. In 2016, 58 percent of internet users around the world were buying online; this jumped to 63 percent in 2019 and, accelerated by lockdowns in response to COVID-19, should reach more than 65 percent in 2021.[8] As captured in the chart below, an astounding 83 percent of the buying process now occurs with no seller involved. This percentage will only keep growing.

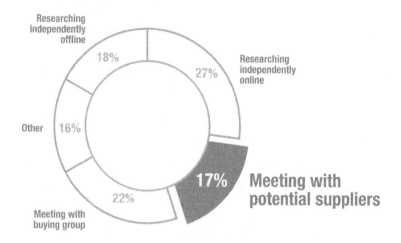

Source: 2020 Gartner The Future of Sales in 2025 Report

7   Lisa Ellis, Jeffrey Saret, and Peter Weed, "BYOD: From Company-Issued to Employee-Owned Devices," McKinsey & Company *Telecommunications, Media, and Technology Practice* No. 20 Recall, June 2012, https://www.mckinsey.com/~/media/mckinsey/dotcom/client_service/high%20tech/pdfs/byod_means_so_long_to_company-issued_devices_march_2012.ashx.

8   "Digital Buyer Penetration Worldwide from 2016 to 2021," *Statista*, accessed February 5, 2019, https://www.statista.com/statistics/261676/digital-buyer-penetration-worldwide.

Social media now influences online business buying as well. Our studies at Engage Selling show that social media, implemented effectively, can speed up closing rates by as much as 51 percent; it achieves this by increasing convenience, availability, speed, and access.

In a digitized world, few care from where products and supplies ship, as long as they arrive in one piece and within a timeline that would have been hard to imagine just a short time ago. Even in the supply chain "reshoring discussions" I'm having with manufacturing clients as I write this book in late 2020, few care where their suppliers are based as long as the supply chain is secure and backed up with alternative sources. Time and access dominate location in importance. Buyers simply expect to connect with the right person for the right help and on the right timeline. **Today's buyer is always "on" and expects the same of you.**

We should all understand our customers' service expectations because we demand the same levels of care ourselves. We call cable providers and other utilities at all hours of the day, expecting they will fall over themselves to meet our needs. T-Mobile has embraced this "always-on" mentality by organizing customer service teams into geographic pods that align with the time zones and cultures of the states they serve. This way, no matter when a customer calls, the team in their region is ready and available to help; everyone gets top service during the hours that suit them best.

Even though we understand and embrace this shift as consumers, far too many of us in the B2B world seem to have fallen woefully behind in adapting to this change. In 2020 many of us could only respond in shock to how fast such change poured into our markets. **Even now many dismiss ubiquity as a B2C buying phenomenon; in so doing they miss the point—oh, and the money from potential sales.** One client recently saw business fall away because its salesperson failed to embrace an "always-on" and "everywhere-on" mindset. This organization does business primarily with other organizations in North America and follows a traditional nine-to-five schedule. Using videoconferencing, this salesperson had been leading a buyer through the sales process. As he closed in on a sale, he discovered that while his contact was based in North America, the division head resided in the Netherlands, and the parent company's headquarters were in China.

The seller proved ill-equipped to manage multiple contacts across different time zones. Even worse, he committed a fatal error: being unwilling to go the extra mile. He had no interest in placing a call at 6:00 a.m. to reach decision makers during what would have been the middle of their afternoon; to this seller time zones were the customer's problem. This approach is not customer-centric; in fact, it's customer-repellent!

Because this salesperson refused to adapt to needs of customers in multiple worldwide locations, the company missed out. How might you avoid a similar fate?

A smart client with whom we work overcomes such setbacks by staggering the inside sales team's hours based on the industries with whom they work most. Those that service construction, fleet owners, and landscapers start their day at 5:00 a.m. because decision makers in those camps tend to be early birds. Those that target manufacturing come in at 8:00 a.m. because they can reach buyers during more traditional work hours. And those that focus on hospitality education and healthcare start a little later but stick around until 7:00 p.m. because these buyers tend to be more accessible outside "traditional" hours. This flexible work schedule ensures my client reaches more of its network and engages in more meaningful conversations with buyers than can any competitors.

"Always-On" Is Already Here

Meeting the needs of the "always-on" buyer is no option; you must come through in a big, bold way to stay relevant in the new landscape. Consider the experience of computer maker Dell, the first to offer online and buy-by-phone business products—they dominated for quite a stretch. This convenience, once novel, has since swept across the B2C landscape. This unyielding attentiveness is why Amazon keeps pulverizing competitors in a dizzying array of markets.

As first discussed in chapter 1, "Amazonification" of the marketplace is well underway, and no one is exempt. **When choosing a supplier, "always-on" wins.** In fact, Amazon itself is penetrating the B2B world. It recently released a private-label motor oil to be sold not only to consumers but also to quick-lube chains and car dealerships, and it is competing directly with office suppliers, electronics manufacturers, and tooling companies—all with this signature "always-on" convenience. This signals a potential move to partner with—or buy—operators to provide Amazon-branded oil changes. This may sound extreme, but it's up to us to meet and exceed this "always-on" expectation—or be crushed under those who will.

Customer-Centric Alignment

Being Right on the Money means wholly refocusing your company processes to target how your *customer* defines success, rather than measuring it by what you'd like to achieve. For example, sellers across industries now offer buyers direct online access to their inventory systems so, on their own time, they can scope out what's available and choose products that fit their needs. We've already seen this with airlines, where anyone can now view and choose available seats. It's also happening in the industrial supply, pharmaceutical, medical supply, and chemical arenas: buyers can log in, see volumes of product available, check prices, and place an order. A company can expedite this process even further when customers can link to a minimum within their own inventory, so when product levels drop to a certain threshold, the system automatically orders more.

Clearhill Enterprises developed their own automated system to keep buyers happy. The company owns and operates children's rides and amusements across the United Kingdom, the kind you find in malls or outside grocery stores. These generate money for the businesses where they're located through a revenue-sharing model. Of course, none of this works if machines break down. So Clearhill installed an automatic monitoring and tracking system on every machine; if one goes down, they dispatch a technician to fix it promptly. As a result, buyers need not report issues, and since technicians address problems immediately, both parties mitigate lost revenue.

When systems like these align with sites that are customer-friendly and easy to navigate and order from, the result is engagement and increased buying. In a study of around ten thousand US-based consumers, Temkin Group found that **86 percent of customers who enjoyed a great experience claimed they would likely return**, as opposed to 13 percent of those who received subpar customer service.[9] Rosetta determined that **"engaged and satisfied customers buy 50 percent more frequently, spend 200 percent more each year, and are five times more likely to display brand loyalty."**[10] As you can see, you must start strategizing how to better align with customer expectations and give buying the boost it needs.

An easy way to create this alignment is to first look at customer satisfaction and sales.

Most companies with whom I work conduct customer satisfaction surveys, although a disappointing few do anything with results. They want customers to *feel* they have a voice, but because this outreach usually happens only once a year, and since nothing happens with the information, the research proves virtually useless. Feedback from customers is essential if you hope to anticipate—rather than just respond to—buyer needs.

Beyond simply capturing a moment in time, your goal should be to maintain an ever-evolving spotlight on current customer experiences. Doing so provides the requisite intelligence to understand changing requirements in the marketplace so we can, in turn, modify how we do business—before our industries, in exasperation, demand it.

---

9   Bruce Temkin, "The Ultimate CX Infographic, 2018," *Experience Matters* by Qualtrics, October 2, 2018.
10 Nikki Gilliland, "17 Stats That Show Why CX is So Important," *Econconsultancy*, July 20, 2017, https://econsultancy.com/17-stats-that-show-why-cx-is-so-important.

A national oil company client of mine in the Middle East had long been a leader in employing traditional, by-the-book customer satisfaction surveys. They conducted this research each year, included a net promoter score, and adhered closely to classic *Harvard Business Review* best practices. In spite of this rigor, sellers admitted to me they never translated the information into more customer-centric business practices, and buyers turned out to be less satisfied than they indicated on the survey. Customers pressed for better pricing, raised other issues, and, ultimately, bolted from the company for the competition.

I suggested evolving their research a step further. When customer satisfaction results came in, they could study them to spot trends and then powwow over such issues with buyers. I proposed they dig deeper with follow-up questions: *What are your opinions on this? How do you think we should tackle this issue? Which of these areas are most interesting or relevant to you?*

By sharing and asking, they established a high-level audience with important buyers. Immediately, senior-level decision makers sought to be involved in subsequent meetings. Sellers found themselves before people heretofore out of reach and, during those get-togethers, uncovered countless interesting initiatives their clients were undertaking.

My client opened up conversations on topics unrelated to selling products; in fact, meetings seemed more like advisory sessions. Still, those discussions gave them an inside scoop. One buyer described a new green mandate to reduce engine function and emissions. This insight led my client to anticipate a new business need: to help clients convert diesel engines into cleaner-burning fuel ones.

In pursuing a new strategy, my client quickly earned a favorable pole position, well ahead of important trends. They could now not only gauge how buyers saw their business but also track new ideas and challenges and proactively address them before formal needs arose.

You can start small. Ask a simple question about the biggest problems your buyers face. Doing so can help you anticipate—and win.

The Key to Ease of Buying? Balance

You must figure out how to create a clear, uncluttered path between your customers and what you're selling. But when it comes to giving customers what they want, customer centricity demands balance. Gut-level wisdom suggests the more options you offer, the better, but this can backfire. **Too many choices at any stage in the customer life cycle may present a recipe for escalating costs and buyer frustration. In short, over offering can slaughter a brand and hurt a buyer's ability to make a choice.** The following example illustrates just how dangerous such a mistake can be to your bottom line:

Recently, Engage Selling launched a powerful new customer-journey mapping program. While implementing this tool at a major global energy company, we uncovered surprising insights about the company's ordering process. My client offered five different paths to place orders—phone, email, a direct online portal, EDI link, and fax. Buyers could also request what they sought from three different contacts: a distribution sales rep, an in-house account manager, or a general 1-800 customer service line. While my client felt confident they were doing the right thing by offering so many choices, this excess of options created only irritation and delays. A typical email exchange with a customer looked like this:

> *Customer: "I would like to order four pallets of your product."*
> *Seller: "We offer five different formats to place an order ... which would you like?"*
> *Customer: "Whichever we used last time."*
> *Seller (reaching the buyer after three callback attempts): "We shipped it to you four times last month and to four different warehouses. You also ordered in four different ways. Which one do you prefer?"*
> *Customer: "I don't know. Why are you making this so difficult? Just ship what I ordered last time and how I ordered it last time."*

Exchanges like this frustrate both buyer and seller, make delays inevitable, and lead to avoidable mistakes. Every aspect of this interaction—including the confusion and frequent calls—drives up the cost to serve the buyer and heightens the risk they'll leave.

In this case offering so many options spawned a near-crippling level of inconsistency and complexity. Only online orders could be processed immediately. Each other system followed a unique process with varying levels of speed and accuracy, with the consequence that orders often needed to be reentered by hand! The process could take days to complete, especially for orders placed before a long weekend. And for every ordering option except online ordering, my client had no way to measure results.

With all the challenges caused by this process, you may ask: *Why did they do this*? The answer is simple: to make buying convenient. They assumed customers desired more choice, when instead they wanted to order quickly and receive consistent results. **You need not create an endless array of buying options; instead, concentrate on providing the *right* choices.**

Amazon demonstrates the benefits of limiting choice. They offer one ordering option and a single route of communication. While this may seem annoying or inconvenient should your instinct be to pick up the phone, having one means of contact allows for issues to be more easily routed to the right person and thus resolved more quickly. And since everything is captured electronically, any customer-facing employee can bring up buyer information and relay it instantly.

The bottom line? **The customer may not always be right, but you must always do right by the customer.** In this case this means building processes that lead the buyer seamlessly through the best possible experience, even if this means offering fewer unnecessary bells and whistles.

Returning to our option-overloading client, how did we make it easier for the customer to buy? We shifted to a single ordering system that generates consistent and measurable data. With no more temperamental templates, emails, or faxes, the client offers accurate order processing, faster delivery, and a mere fraction of the mistakes. Now they're meeting customer expectations where it actually matters!

As a bonus the move to a simpler system yielded significant cost savings. The company's five-channel ordering system required two-and-a-half full-time employees to manage—conservatively, at least $100,000 in salaries and benefits. A simpler system could save the company those salaries, or allow them to move those employees to more profitable areas of the business.

Getting Time on Your Side

Thriving in the new landscape and being Right on the Money is all about saving time for your buyer. Meet them when they want and how they want, with products and services they need. Offer speed and accuracy of aligned systems. Connect them with people necessary to spur confident decision-making. Do all of these as part of time-based branding, and you'll close more sales and generate repeat business.

But it's not just about *when*—the *how* and *what* count too. With so much information out there, you must make sure you're participating in the conversation, giving buyers content they need, and weighing in on what they choose to share.

Chapter 3:

CRITICAL MASS INFLUENCE

While meeting with a group of almost painfully traditional sellers in the oil and gas industry, I argued the case for mass influence as a critical factor in generating sales. One older gentleman tipped back, rubbed his palms together, and said: "Colleen, you're forgetting the key point: people still buy from people."

I paused for a minute and replied, "You know what? You're absolutely right. Sales *is* still a people business. It's just that there are now ten or more times as many people involved."

The personal aspect of sales has always been vital. What has changed, though, is that sales today are influenced heavily by what I call *Critical Mass Influence*: the vector of people affecting your ability to complete transactions within a tight timeframe. Thirty years ago, when I started selling, we focused our efforts on a relatively small group of buyers inside each account.

Only one or two people, such as a trusted advisor or peer referral, influenced any sale.

Today we sell to millions by reaching populations measured in billions and in economies measured in trillions. Tens—if not hundreds—of times more people play roles in the sales cycle, many of whom you'll never meet nor influence directly.

People today stay deeply interconnected—constantly talking online and offline, whether you're tuned in or not. **Every person in your market wields power in today's marketplace. Their conversations and the content they generate—accurate or wildly false or misleading—directly strengthen or impede your chances of securing a sale.** And while your buyer makes the final decision about whether or not to choose you, each influencer—inside the company and outside, online and off—determines whether you find a seat at the table. For this reason, you must connect to each player, and you must adhere to a customer-centric approach to sales.

You're certain to be part of conversations, whether the speaker is a lifelong friend or a complete stranger. Some may sing your praises; others might toss sharp barbs. Still others may serve up commentary that veers wildly away from the truth. Years ago, politically incensed reviewers attacked every Red Hen Restaurant they encountered, propagating volumes of fake news in the process. It's up to you to inject yourself into these conversations and to help mold them to your advantage. The best sales teams understand that while they cannot control every person in their market, they can employ Critical Mass Influence to leverage them and to link with everyone playing a part. Doing this well requires understanding the origins of this particular landscape shift.

Grappling with a Low-Trust Environment

Today buyers rely on each other to arrive at decisions. In the B2B sphere, if buyers fail to find multiple references and citations attesting to your value—along with resources and case studies showcasing your successes—they'll never pick up the phone to call you, nor answer when you call. Why? Because beyond being pressed for time, they feel no reason to trust you. According to the Edelman Trust Barometer, which surveys thousands worldwide, the general public's trust of CEOs sits at just 37 percent, and only 52 percent "trust business to do what is right."[11] According to LinkedIn's 2018 "State of Sales," 51 percent of buyers ranked *trust* as the top factor they desire in sales professionals—even though, as we know, few actually find us trustworthy.[12]

Buyers have neither the time nor the stomach to deal with those they don't trust. They see risk everywhere. Customers today trust in their own truth, formed independently and driven as much by emotion as by reason. Remember: buyers spend only 17 percent of today's sales cycle talking to sellers. To make up the balance, buyers source information from peer groups and their own research. They allow sellers no opportunity to shape how they feel about a product; instead, they first decide for themselves, based on the experiences and opinions of others. Let's explore the impact of these external forces and nail down how to maximize the positive effects in your sales process.

11   Matthew Harrington, "Survey: People's Trust Has Declined in Business, Media, Government, and NGOs," *Harvard Business Review*, January 16, 2017, https://hbr.org/2017/01/survey-peoples-trust-has-declined-in-business-media-government-and-ngos.

12   "The State of Sales 2018," LinkedIn, accessed January 6, 2019, https://business.linkedin.com/sales-solutions/b2b-sales-strategy-guides/the-state-of-sales-2018.

Power to the People

My own research in multiple industries over twenty years confirms the adage: "Buyers believe buyers first." Office managers believe office managers first; CIOs trust other CIOs; and sellers turn to sellers. Believing those you perceive to be most like you represents a core behavioral trait. For this reason, trusted recommendations and referrals from peers endure as the single biggest influencer in the buying process. Alas, this also presents five complicating factors with which sellers tangle every day:

1. Access to top buyers is limited by time and their lack of inclination to meet with us.
2. Buyers insulate themselves with influencers, so we must first win over these influencers to carve a path to the buyer.
3. More people than ever participate in decision-making, and post-pandemic my clients share that new players with whom they've never interacted are showing up in the process, thus dramatically changing *who* they need to influence.
4. Direct referrals from trusted sources are becoming scarce as buyers agonize over liability and risk exposure.
5. Everyone in your own company affects Critical Mass Influence, even if their roles are not customer-facing.

So how do you counteract these factors? You must take Critical Mass Influence into your own hands.

Consider my experience. Recently I needed to purchase a new light for video production work. My social media team, headed by Lisa Larter (a trusted referral source), pointed me toward a certain vendor. When I pulled up Amazon for a price comparison, the people vector began to reshape my buying process.

I scrolled through buyer reviews and first-person feedback about the light I wanted. Amazon pointed out that "people who bought X also bought Y," which led me to check out competitors and their offerings. After an hour of connecting disparate dots and soliciting advice from complete strangers, I bought my light and added two extra items to my shopping cart. Overall, as many as two dozen people played some role in my buying decision—none of whom I spoke to directly. And, interestingly, I found myself forming opinions based more on the *quantity* of reviews than their quality. While Lisa offered a solid reference, digging into opinions from a dozen others—who I also came to regard as peers—proved even more powerful and persuasive.

In the Absence of Trust, Volume Wins

Why did that happen? Because of a simple truth: an effect multiplies when it appears in aggregate.

That's Critical Mass Influence at work. And sellers must master these multipliers to attract new opportunities with influencers and buyers. Today volume is power. The more people talk about you, the more influence you wield with buyers (existing and potential) and their influencers. Consider your own buying behavior. You likely attach more weight to the number of stars a company boasts and the volume of reviewers who contributed to that rank on Google, Amazon, or Yelp than to written feedback. Now look at what happens when you apply these principles to your own enterprise.

Tulips & Maple Inc., a corporate catering client, wanted to leverage their firm's legacy to build bigger brand buzz. Their solution? Tap their loyal, happy, clients whom they felt would gladly help them. When asked, their clients wrote Google reviews about them. Inbound inquiries increased dramatically, and a simple gesture created a virtuous circle. Harness this technique for your business. Showcase reviews, case studies, testimonials, and quotes from customers on your websites, social media profiles, and in industry forums. It is easy, if you do it deliberately and cement it as an ongoing part of your sales process. Phillip Brown, CEO of Tulips and Maple, stated, "We also harnessed a global firm that excels in social media practices and processes to drive our messaging outward. Sales have quintupled in the past five years."

All this blossomed out of a simple gesture. To harness the same technique, showcase reviews, case studies, testimonials, and quotes from customers on your website, on social media profiles, and in industry forums. It's not difficult—but it must be a deliberate, concrete, and ongoing part of your sales process.

Profiting from Critical Mass Influence

As the graphic illustrates, you build Critical Mass Influence by broadening your circle around a customer and taking advantage of the compounding power of multiple points of contact. You achieve this in four key ways. First, you reinforce contact with existing buyers—those already using your products or services. You then reach out to all internal influencers inside prospect accounts who have the ear of potential buyers. Third, you recognize and exploit your own colleagues and employees as ambassadors to further broaden your brand; in essence, each part of your business becomes a profit center. Finally, you interact with "strangers"—those on the periphery to whom your buyers pay attention, including people in your networks, in associations, and on social media, as well as journalists, consultants, and trade analysts. Such outsiders may not be part of the organization, per se, but they *do* drive sales.

Let's delve into each group.

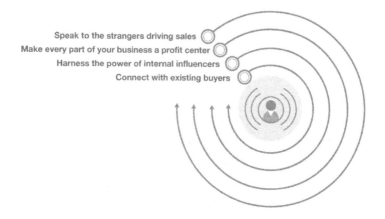

Speak to the strangers driving sales
Make every part of your business a profit center
Harness the power of internal influencers
Connect with existing buyers

Connect with All Existing Buyers

To leverage Critical Mass Influence, you must maximize your network of current customers. You do this by connecting with them on all the platforms they frequent and leveraging the good-will developed with them over time. As much as trust has faltered and negativity permeates the world at large, your buyers will typically speak kindly of you and what you offer. You regularly receive positive feedback, whether your customer ends a phone call by gushing, "I love the work you're doing," or replies to an email saying, "Thanks, this has been really helpful." Too few

of us capitalize on this goodwill to strengthen our networks—
we leave the positivity sitting there instead of employing it to
boost our community size and market image. You must learn
to indulge a knee-jerk reaction of sorts: **as soon as someone
says anything complimentary, ask them to connect and tell
you more.** Digging just a bit deeper will reveal whether or not
there's meat behind the compliments and make it clear if you
can use it to attract the attention of others.

Getting Right on the Money: Quick Tip

Here are eight key steps to make your networking efforts Right
on the Money:

1. Build your community by connecting with all buyers
   and client contacts wherever they hang out online.
   While each industry is different, the best formula usually involves some combination of LinkedIn, industry and
   trade forums, Facebook, and Twitter.
2. Build goodwill by endorsing your customer contacts and
   highlighting their success and expertise in working with
   you. Always give first before asking.
3. Ask if you can share your success story with others. If your
   customers agree, type up a case study that puts them in
   the limelight and send it to them for approval.
4. Ask customers to share feedback on Google, LinkedIn,
   and other relevant platforms. Those kudos generate the
   kind of buzz that makes you look like a rising star.

5. Ask if you can convert customers' comments and experiences into a case study or formal feature on your website. When prospects read stories from "people like me," this reinforces sales-friendly perceptions.
6. Find customers willing to have you showcase in a video their businesses and the success you've helped them achieve. Video resonates deeply with influencers, as they can literally see themselves (or others just like them) in the story.
7. Work with clients to create a virtual or in-person presentation or panel at an industry meeting or trade show. This demonstrates to attendees how your product or service made a positive impact on their peers.
8. Return the favor by endorsing their work and promoting it generously inside your own networks.

In building your influence community, be sure to pick a variety of customer experiences, markets, and solutions so you highlight the full portfolio of what you offer. This may sound too simple to be true, but the fact remains: most customers don't *buy* more simply because they don't know you *offer* more. When did you last initiate a deep conversation with your client about everything you offer in the context of how their peers buy?

My client Snelling Paper and Sanitation crafted a highly effective strategy to share information about their entire portfolio to each customer without being overwhelming—on the surface no small task, given that their catalogue boasts well over one thousand products! On every sales call, they gathered and showcased "people who bought X also bought Y" recommendations and parlayed this show-and-tell into a 5-percent jump in sales. It's little different than asking, "Would you like fries with that?" but backed by business intelligence based on people's preferences.

After you tap your existing network of customers, you can then reach into the broader community of strangers who can also influence your buyer.

Harness the Power of Internal Influencers

Your next important source of influencers is the pool of those with whom your buyers insulate themselves through the buying process. Ask yourself:

1. Who are my buyer's key direct reports—one or two people exerting a real impact on decisions?
2. Who is the backup or replacement should my primary contact be unavailable?
3. Who is my buyer's likely successor?
4. Who are likely stakeholders? While they may not use the product directly, if it affects their work, they're influencers too.
5. Who else in the organization is affected—positively or negatively—by the solutions you provide? They could all have the ear of your buyer.
6. Does your product promise a financial benefit? If yes, the finance team becomes an influencer.
7. Is your prospect a smaller, privately owned business? If yes, the owners could influence the buyer as well.
8. Does your solution affect your prospect's customers? If yes, then sales and service staff could be influencers.

9. Does the buyer use a consulting company for advisory services? If yes, add them to your list of possible influencers.

With the names of influencers in hand, you can paint a clear
picture of your buyer's community. Accessing this community
may not alone secure any sale, but this makes it no less vital to
your progress, because it may well at least snag you a seat at the
table. Don't make the common mistake of thinking you should
only connect with the most senior levels inside client accounts;
all employees whose work is affected by the products you sell
are important influencers in some way and could ultimately rise
up through the organization to become buyers. Building and
nurturing a network of them now ensures you maintain access to
the best information from the broadest sources possible. Thus,
you must ensure you reach out to these audiences in the locations where they hang out—and keep in mind where they hang
out might be changing!

Even before the pandemic canceled large trade shows in 2020,
a client shared their intent to step away from participating in trade
shows at which they'd been a fixture for years. Why? Last year
they spent $100,000 making their typical rounds, but their target
buyers and influencers turned out to be no-shows. For the future
they'll invest instead in tracking down this missing community
and looking for new ways to connect online, in trade publications,
and at other smaller events that their clients are frequenting.

Make Every Part of Your Business a Profit Center
One colossal misstep business leaders make when striving to be
Right on the Money is to frame customer relationships as sales

department initiatives. Everyone—from delivery people to folks in accounting, from executives to junior salespeople—plays an active role in transforming relationships into profit.

In this case what do I mean by *active*? You've heard the naval expression "All hands on deck." This neatly sums up how teams of people with diverse responsibilities unite behind a common objective: to keep a ship afloat through turbulent seas. In the new business landscape, leaders must also issue this call, because it's the only way to be there for the buyer in ways they've grown to expect.

Salespeople prospect and sell your product or service, but everyone in your organization needs to jump behind selling your *brand* and ensuring revenue translates into profits. Your customer buys from your company, not from you, so every interaction between your customers and your people—from receptionists and truck drivers to senior executives—contributes to (or detracts from) your ability to exert positive influence.

A client in the office supply sector learned this lesson the hard way. In sleuthing why return sales were flagging, my client discovered its product assemblers had developed the unsettling habit of offering very unflattering commentary, out loud, about what the customer just bought—bashing the flimsy material and faulty screws—all while they installed the product onsite! With the brand tarnished and the customers not wanting to be part of this company's community, building Critical Mass Influence became an impossible dream—and ongoing attempts to grow the customer failed. After retraining installers and coaching them on customer communication, my client gradually turned the situation around.

From this example you can see why you must give all employees the tools and initiative to do the following:

- connect with their contacts in a meaningful way;
- promote values for which your company stands;
- ask for client referrals;
- build relationships; and
- spot new sales opportunities.

Being Right on the Money—and setting a course for customer centricity—happens when every member of your crew plays an active part in growing the company's network. This is about much more than handing out business cards.

A client in the industrial supply arena included its whole team in building Critical Mass Influence. Their team of drivers held three jobs over and above product delivery: listening to the customer's needs, wishes, interests, and experiences; reporting back on what they heard; and building their own community of contacts. The sales department used that information to modify prospecting and follow-up activity to better meet needs of their territory. Here are some other examples:

1. In Canada, sales executive Tim Welch routinely asks his CEO to introduce members of her network to salespeople in the field.

2. Pet supply company RC Pets encourages all pet-owning staff (and that's most of them!) to outfit pets in company gear and then photograph them for advertising, brand promotion, and social media initiatives.

3. A global financial services client leads all employees through a social media compliance workshop that informs them how to use a variety of media to positively influence the market and their followers. Once this training is complete, they encourage these folks to employ their personal platforms and networks of friends and family as an influence tool. This extends the company's reach exponentially.

4. Three of my clients work in particularly impressive facilities. Each builds their office space and people into their Critical Mass Influence strategy. They bring prospects to their facilities to meet the team with whom they'll be working. Next, they open their spaces for events, so vendors, suppliers, and business partners can take advantage of a top-notch place to meet. They even donate their facilities for community events and ask employees to lend a hand. All these strategies increase their influence in the market and on its decision makers.

5. The spare parts and tooling department at Orbitform regularly shares posts from the company's LinkedIn page and from blogs on their own personal pages to increase reach and drive inbound inquiries. Their departments sales have increased 30% a month over the last year.

When you make all employees influencers, you focus a vast wave of resources on keeping your business growing and thriving—even in a tough market.

Speak to the Strangers Driving Sales

If you know a myriad of strangers have injected your company into conversations—in the process boosting or scuttling your sales—you must abandon any shyness or modesty and chime in on conversations wherever they're happening. Some disagree with this position; I face pushback from many in traditional industries when I promote the merits of social media. As I see it, if buyers and potential buyers congregate on these platforms, you need to show up too.

One client recently called me "crazy" for suggesting they build a presence on Twitter. In frustration they barked, "Our clients are old school; they'd never follow us on Twitter!" When I logged in to confirm their assertion, I discovered the company's lack of presence had done nothing to stop buyers and prospects from chattering behind the company's digital back. Hundreds of discussions, good and bad, had been happening over the years in various online venues; my client had just been no part of them. With no formal presence, my client had disinvited itself. Buyers praising my client online received no positive reinforcement, so nobody could capitalize on huge volumes of good news. Worse, complaints also fell on deaf ears. What happens when angry buyers feel ignored? They grow louder, and when such messaging becomes amplified—with no strategy to counter it—sales suffer.

The only way to leverage the massive impact of people-generated content—buyer reviews, Facebook posts, tweets, YouTube comments, and more—is to participate in these conversations on the platforms where they're happening. Never indulge the folly of dismissing such channels as irrelevant, which is akin to pretending your buyer can't see you merely because you've covered your eyes.

How else can you create and nurture a positive influence? Get your whole team involved.

In the next chapter, I cover one more approach to harness the power of Critical Mass Influence. You must consistently participate in conversations buyers are having and leave a noteworthy mark in content they consume. You do this by understanding and acknowledging that *all* news—no matter who generates it or even whether it's true or not—contributes to Critical Mass Influence. And this means it's time to use news to your advantage.

Chapter 4

CONTROLLING YOUR OWN STORY

Amid a massive rethink of how we carry on business with each other in a post pandemic world, we must also grapple with a shift that has, for years, been slowly and quietly at play: **Today your buyer *sees you* before you see them.** Upon noticing you they begin to shape their own story about who you are, what you offer, and how they feel about you. This happens whether or not you help shape your character in this story, so it's best that you do. Let's look at why and how.

You may have already sensed this sea change in buyer behavior, and data bears this out. In their recent "State of B2B Procurement Study," Accenture found that 94 percent of B2B buyers conduct at least some research online before they make a purchase.[13] Further, according to Sirius Decisions, 67 percent

---

13 "2014 State of B2B Procurement Study: Uncovering the Shifting Landscape in B2B Commerce," Accenture Interactive, https://www.accenture.com/

of buying today happens digitally. And to repeat and amplify an important stat from chapter 3, more than 83 percent of a buyer's time is spent researching solutions and talking to contacts, peers, and advisors.

Think about what this means for how you do business.

Your customer reads about you. They learn what others think you offer. They talk to others about their experiences doing business with you. They engage with your content. They research your products or services and evaluate your claims about them. And when they are ready—and only then—they may contact you. Much of this activity, this new buying process, happens wholly without you.

This shift doesn't mean you can now sit back and wait for buyers to toss bags of money into your lap. You play a new role: to set the stage for when buyers may be ready to give you a sale and to create the winning conditions that make possible a "buyer-finds-seller" moment. As a seller you must now determine where your "people" reside, develop a deep understanding of what they care about, and then create and spread content that attracts and engages them.

To do this well, you must stay on top of everything published about you and your company—both good and bad. You must jump into the conversation by interacting with your buyer and your buyer's influencers on all their preferred channels. This will only happen, though, if you do the legwork—an imposing task at the best of times and a bigger challenge when stretched

---

t20150624T211502__w__/us-en/_acnmedia/Accenture/Conversion-Assets/
DotCom/Documents/Global/PDF/Industries_15/Accenture-B2B-Procurement-
Study.pdf.

thinner than ever as we continue to struggle to recover from the global pandemic.

Opinions of others influence deeply your buyer's decision to purchase from you. As you track down this buzz, expect to encounter (and accept) the good and the bad—the five-star and the one-star reviews. Whether those appraisals are fair or unfair is unimportant; what matters is that you can't ignore *any* feedback. Instead, you must participate in every conversation, no matter where or when they happen or who starts them.

Setting the Stage and Framing the Conversation

While sellers must keep up with a deluge of information daily, the most successful go beyond simply participating; they *take control* by providing buyers with high-value content across a variety of platforms. What *aren't* they doing? They no longer contact unknown potential buyers directly, in person or by phone. Consider two floundering sellers who learned this lesson the hard way.

First meet Ben, a client with buyers in the finance sector. Ben consistently struggles to make his numbers. His work ethic is beyond question; it's his archaic habits that threaten to render him obsolete. Ben's cold call ratios have steadily dropped over five years, from a conversion rate of ten to one to a paltry 260 to one. When I propose alternative approaches, such as emailing his prospect the high-value content his company produces for its website, he resists. "Cold calls are the only thing that works," he insists, and then adds, "but I guess I could get my son to show me how to use social media." And he wonders why he never makes President's Club for his company!

This example might sound extreme, but in markets with legacy sellers (or with "salty veterans," as sales VP Ryan Wilson tags them), such shortcomings are far from uncommon—and those legacy sellers aren't the only ones struggling today.

This leads me to the second example. Sales Leader Zach complains to me often that his younger sellers waste time hanging out on social media when they should be creating new opportunities by engaging with buyers. Though cultivating an online presence is essential today, Zach, and leaders like him are nevertheless ... *right*! Too many sellers follow no concrete path for employing social media—they're just "hanging out." They haven't learned how to harness the power of LinkedIn, Twitter, Facebook, and other platforms to win customers and business. This *is* a big problem.

Neither type of floundering seller—the legacy player bent on cold-calling, nor the newbie equipped with tools but no road map—need afflict your team. Instead capitalize on the cultural shift by systematically working to be "found" by prospective customers. You do this by engaging in ubiquitous conversations within your sphere of influence so buyers can delve into information about you and your solutions when and where they want. *They* decide to engage with you. Understand what drives that decision: *familiarity*. And familiarity comes from ubiquity.

Critical Mass Influence Requires Ubiquity

Buyers won't buy from strangers. Instead, they turn to the salesperson or company they already know and trust, or they seek referrals from their community. **The more a prospect sees you and hears from you in their community of influence, the more familiar you become—and the more likely you are to capture their business.**

The vast swamp of information your buyers encounter every day is only going to grow, and you must leverage all of it to take full advantage of the Critical Mass Influence you aspire to build. **You must become ubiquitous.**

Create an environment in which people head your way because they're reading great things about you online. Make it so they benefit from high-value, non- "salesy" information you share with the marketplace. This begins when you start showing up everywhere.

Every day I share this Right on the Money advice with sellers: "Simply being on social media, sending an email, or making a call isn't enough. Your team must produce, publish, and share information from numerous sources, and on a variety of platforms, to increase ubiquity in the marketplace."

Ubiquity requires three elements to be successful: diversity of platforms, diversity of content, and relevance to your market. Success comes from balancing these components; those who fail often focus on one but neglect the others. So, for example, if you have:

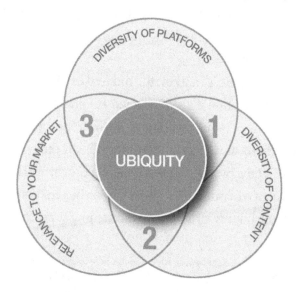

1. A diversity of platforms and content, but such content is not relevant to your market, you are *invisible.*
2. Diversity of content relevant to your market, but you neglect to promote it across a diverse number of platforms, you lack *volume.*
3. Relevant content published on many platforms, but this content lacks diversity in its messaging, you are *stagnant.*

When you maintain a diverse platform with a variety of content sources relevant to your market, you become ubiquitous and thus impossible to ignore. So how do companies and sellers achieve ubiquity?

The Triad Tempo

I recommend using the Triad Tempo as a simple way to achieve ubiquity. Start by choosing three different platforms—such as Twitter, LinkedIn, YouTube, Instagram, or Facebook. Don't decide randomly or settle only on channels you use most. It matters little where *you* like to hang out; you must go to where your customers gather.

In today's business market, the old real estate adage of "location, location, location" is still crucial. If I shared that you could find 75 percent of your customers in the room next door, you would run there now. Social media *is* that room, so you *must* be there. A study by IDC found that 75 percent of B2B buyers and 84 percent of companies' most senior buyers employ social media in their buying process.[14] Maintaining a professional and

---

14 Kathleen Schaub, "Social Buying Meets Social Selling: How Trusted Networks Improve the Purchase Experience," IDC White Paper, April 2014, https://

active social profile is extra important—if people cannot see you, they assume you either don't exist or have become irrelevant.

Once you've chosen your three platforms, the next step is to create and publish three types of content:

1. **Original, high-value content.**
   Write an article or create a video in which you offer insightful and forward-thinking views on current events relevant to your industry. You could also share a thought-provoking how-to tip as a status update or tweet. This showcases your thought leadership or expertise in a particular area. Checking this off your list can be as easy as reposting your company's content to your personal pages—complete with a line or two of original commentary, of course. Chevron Lubricant sellers routinely repost updates from their corporate LinkedIn page. When Emirates National Oil Company posted a press release about using solar power to run their gas stations, corporate sellers in many divisions updated their personal pages with quotes from executive leadership and plans for the rollout. My clients in highly regulated industries or in tightly controlled publicly traded companies routinely borrow preapproved content from the marketing department and post it as their own.

2. **Content from other sources.**
   This could be a timely news article certain to make your customers take notice, witty anecdotes or success stories

---

business.linkedin.com/content/dam/business/sales-solutions/global/en_US/c/pdfs/idc-wp-247829.pdf.

from other customers, or a pertinent product announcement. Put this content out there with one sentence of commentary promoting why you think your buyer or network should give it a look. While personal touches aren't critical, **distributing highly valuable information *is*—even if you or your company didn't create it**. For example, when Tesla shared an announcement about a new electric freightliner truck, clients of mine in the oil industry made sure to pass it on via social media, along with a question about whether their fleet customers might be interested in such a vehicle. This question inspired more conversations than usual—and more opportunities for sales meetings. Similarly, a smart agricultural consultant I know, Wes Anderson, constantly posts articles both *for* and *against* genetically modified organisms, or GMOs, just to stimulate conversation, regardless of which side of the argument his clients fall on. In doing so he captures a broader share of the market than his competitors.

3. **Comment on—and share—your customer's/prospect's articles or posts.**

   This could be a simple question, a thought-provoking statement, or a congratulatory note. What's important is that you let your customers know you're listening to them. People often worry that following clients and sharing their information could be misconceived as stalking—it's not. Buyers put content out there in hopes it will get noticed; had they wanted it hidden, they wouldn't have published it. By noticing and sharing, you build rapport. And when the time comes to buy, you'll be top of mind.

Repeat each of these three action points three times a week, and you'll soon see how the Triad Tempo works for you.

When engagement is plotted effectively, sales are almost guaranteed to increase. In a study of more than ten thousand companies, CSO Insights found total quota attainment rises when more sellers are online, being social, and producing information for which buyers are looking. While average quota attainment was 57.7 percent across the board, organizations that reported that their content strategy needed significant work realized below-average rates of quota attainment, with only 51 percent of sellers hitting targets. Those who stated their content strategy met or exceeded expectations saw higher-than-average rates, with 70 percent of sellers hitting quotas. **Put simply, the Triad Tempo increases sales while focusing sellers on vital information and insights, so they don't spend wasteful hours surfing all day.**

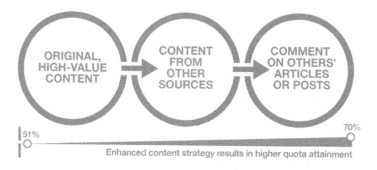

ORIGINAL, HIGH-VALUE CONTENT → CONTENT FROM OTHER SOURCES → COMMENT ON OTHERS' ARTICLES OR POSTS

51% ——————————————— 70%

Enhanced content strategy results in higher quota attainment

My clients' data tells a similar story. One started targeting information online and via email and saw five times greater engagement with potential buyers, a 40-percent faster close rate, and a 31-percent boost in closing ratios. Those numbers speak volumes.

Another client experienced the impact of sharing high-quality content even before social media became popular. Back then I advised this company's executives on the importance of adding value by propagating personal and professional content. As we sat in their conference room brainstorming how they could reach clients, I asked if they were doing anything that might pique client interest. It turned out that they were sponsoring an art gallery opening.

One grumbled, "I can tell you one thing for certain, though: none of my CEO and CFO clients are going to show up at an art show."

"That's fine," I said. "It doesn't matter if they come. You just need a reason to reach out and something of value to share."

Doubtful but figuring he had nothing to lose, this executive sent his clients an invitation. And he was half right: every single invitee declined. But six CFOs also thanked him for thinking of them and suggested they get together for a meeting. Even with no takers for the event, the invitation provided an excuse to stay in front of buyers (and the bosses of those buyers) and to further cultivate those relationships.

As mentioned, this example took place before social media, and things have changed a bit since. That's why the Triad Tempo will ensure your time is profitable, regardless of the platforms your clients have embraced.

Here's a quick breakdown of what and how much to post:

- Share three pieces of your own unique content, three pieces of other content, and comments on three posts.
- Do this three times a week.

- And do this on three different platforms.

Wondering how you'll find time to build this tempo? Let's talk about optimization. You can take a few simple steps to incorporate regular communication and engagement into your professional and personal life, making the process relatively quick and painless—and seriously productive.

Use Your Downtime Effectively

As I reflect on sellers who make the very most of their downtime, a client in the commercial leasing business springs to mind. As one of the company's top three performers, she has mastered connecting with buyers in a way that works for her and for them. She works in a business-to-business environment. Her buyers work nine-to-five, and so does she—and she has a family with several children to whom she "reports" when she leaves the office. But she's realized many of her clients do their research after hours. So, she leaves her LinkedIn app open on her phone in the evening. She'll spend a total of fifteen minutes per night— just a few moments before or after dinner and after the kids have gone to bed—responding to any messages.

She believes it's important to be there when her clients need her. Many times, that's at 8:00 p.m., when they finally find time to check in. By responding promptly, she dramatically increases the chances to score a meeting during regular business hours. She's not a workaholic, and she's not letting the app cut into her family time or delay her bedtime, because sending a quick reply takes so little time. And the benefits far outweigh any additional legwork. A quick response shows she's willing to meet buyers where they're at. And as a result buyers think: "Oh, you're like me. You understand." **This sense of compatibility creates trust—of the utmost importance these days—and encourages ongoing engagement.**

Lori, a top performer at recruiting business Excel HR, devotes her commute time to building important connections. She takes the bus to work and, after she boards, puts in her ear buds and plays soothing music to drown out fellow passengers. Next, she scours websites, LinkedIn pages, and job boards for opportunities. She arrives at the office with a host of items for her team to investigate. Last year she and her colleague produced more in a year than anyone had dreamed possible; this was practically the equivalent of breaking the four-minute mile. And yet she confines all additional research time to her commute—an hour when she'd otherwise be twiddling her thumbs or scrolling through Facebook. It's just enough time to get done what she needs to do. And when she gets home, she's all about her family.

Plenty of sellers harness this strategy: devote free time to align with buyers' needs and to work smarter. One client in the education publishing business knows teachers are the major decision makers when it comes to their products, but they can't respond while in their classrooms. So, the company's sellers send emails and make calls at 9:00 each night, conforming to the buyer's most accessible timeframe.

Doing this well is all about making the most of any extra moments. As you sit in a real or virtual lobby waiting for a meeting to start, use your smartphone to connect and respond on LinkedIn. If you arrive early at an evening event or if you're on a flight with Wi-Fi, use that time to make or strengthen connections. If I'm taking time away from my family to travel for work these days, I'm going to use every moment available to me to maximize client contact. If you are not traveling or commuting much these days, consider using some of the time you would have been driving or waiting in a departure lounge to engage with customers. It doesn't have to take long. The truth is, **when it comes to connecting in a way that counts, you need not move mountains: you just have to *show up*.**

Getting Right on the Money: Quick Tip

With all that technology offers, it's so easy to equip yourself with tools to make your downtime more productive. Here are a few strategies to help you deliver whenever your buyer needs you:

- **Tap into apps.** Make sure your phone is stocked with relevant apps like LinkedIn or access to your CRM portal. The more you can access from your mobile device—and hence hold at your fingertips—the easier it is to make the most of your spare moments. A few years ago, at Dreamforce, Salesforce's annual community conference, company founder Marc Benioff boasted how he can run his entire business from his phone. In fact, he shared that Salesforce found sellers are 40-percent more effective when they're mobile-optimized—thus demonstrating we can all put Marc's strategy to work.
- **Put it all out there.** An effective Triad Tempo requires ready access to information. If you make it easily acces-

sible, you don't need to actively feed it to those looking for it. Maintaining an information-intensive website and active social media presence means your audience can find the information they need whenever they're looking for it. Take full advantage of all platforms on which your buyers are active, with the awareness that if you're not flooding the marketplace with your material, then: a) your competition is taking up that space, making them more visible to buyers than you are, and b) you run the risk of clients stumbling on consumer-generated material that makes the case *against* you. This may seem like a slightly paranoid outlook and approach, but it's necessary in this landscape. You're ensuring buyers can find you wherever—and whenever—they look.

- **Let live chat do the work for you.** Another key shift that's driving the always-on buying expectation in B2B is a pervasive tool already in B2C: live chat applications. Resorts, clothing retailers, and cell phone providers (among others) now offer many customer service options via live chat at any time of the day. **With so much exposure to 24/7 chat options in B2C, buyers have come to expect such contact on the B2B side as well.** It's become an entry-level, basic requirement. In my own company, I saw a return on investment within the first month of implementing live chat, and our closing ratios have improved by 87 percent. Today manufacturing clients, banks, and equipment vendors all use this powerful technology to add to their ubiquity to close multiple sales a month and up to a full 25 percent of their monthly revenue. If they can use this to bolster their Tempo Triad, you can too!

- **Use video.** Every successful client with whom we work reports that video yields the highest response rate of all lead-nurturing and conversion programs. Why? Because videos build trust. When prospects *see* you, they feel they *know* you. Video informs the evolving story buyers are telling about you to themselves and to others. Videos associated with training, interviews, thought leadership, recruiting, business cases, and simple company announcements all do very well. It's never been easier to produce and publish high-quality video—and the rapport and response rates are worth the effort.

Get Creative

Sometimes increasing ubiquity and availability demands that you move beyond social media and technology and plunge into the unorthodox in your thinking. One client in the industrial supply arena became ubiquitous in his market by tapping into an established organization that already operates that way—one you've probably heard of: Amazon.

Amazon had acquired an always-open warehouse for industrial products, but they lacked the fleet necessary to offer timely deliveries. By contrast, my client owned the vehicles Amazon needed and subsequently signed a contract to get these products to Amazon's customers.

Prior to the deal, my client had never considered a round-the-clock schedule. As a relatively small business—a speck compared to their mammoth new partner—they knew they could never *beat* them, but this didn't mean they couldn't *join* them. As a result, they've become the company's last-mile delivery arm, a connection that provides multiple ancillary benefits:

- It provides my client with more exposure, putting them in front of buyers and influencers more often and with more trucks on the road. Think "billboard on wheels." This gives my client the opportunity to sell directly to Amazon customers to whom they're delivering.
- It gives my client the opportunity to broadcast and promote their unique partnership, while Amazon orders keep their trucks full and busy.
- It helps them build and strengthen their relationship with Amazon and to potentially take advantage of new opportunities.
- It has allowed them to hire more drivers and extend the hours of others, contributing to regional employment; this in turn enables them to further promote themselves through job postings and announcements.

Each of these benefits helps my client appear ubiquitous in their market, which in turn garners new opportunities and adds unique value to their business.

Today meeting the buyer where they're at, whether on social media or on the road, is no longer a convenience—it's a critical precondition of the buying experience. Do this and you communicate that you're a customer-centric business; ignore it and you convey quite the opposite. Today's technology makes this ubiquity an expectation rather than mere extra credit; luckily the same tools also help meet this expectation. When you employ any and all resources to make yourself readily available to buyers—from your phone to your website—and seek out new, out-of-the-box strategies, you need not worry your buyer will pass you by for a company with broader presence in the market.

Patience Pays Off

Unparalleled access to information, while making our jobs easier, has also rendered our work more challenging, because buyers no longer take action until they absolutely need to—a reality sellers find very frustrating. Still, persistence pays off. Phil Kaplan, managing director at investment company H2C, recently shared how he'd secured a meeting with a potential buyer after more than a year of reaching out. "I just thought the guy didn't like me," he confided. "When he finally emailed me back, I told him that, because it had been so long since I'd heard from him, I had just assumed he didn't want to do business with me."

Phil's contact told him he simply didn't have an immediate need. "There was no point in responding to say I had nothing. Now I have something, and I knew where to find you." This proved an eye-opening lesson for Phil: silence doesn't mean your buyers are ignoring you; instead they may just be filing valuable information and waiting for the appropriate time to make contact. Remember: trust is built over time. I see many people fail simply because they throw in the towel too soon.

Consistency pays off. When buyers see you at networking events, click through your posts, hear your messages on their voicemails, and read your emails, they start to see you as someone with whom they should engage and to whom they should pay attention. All of this informs the story they tell themselves—and share with others—about you. But getting to this point demands both time and legwork. You build the character in the story others tell of you. You must keep producing to keep yourself heard above the noise—and part of the challenge is to figure out exactly who is involved in the conversation and what you can say to make them take notice.

Chapter 5:

NEW MINDSET FOR A CHANGED LANDSCAPE

I n my last book, *Nonstop Sales Boom,* I promoted what was then sage business development advice: define your ideal buyer and then pursue more just like them. Half a decade later—eons, really, in the annals of sales philosophy—the assumptions that anchored that advice simply don't hold up anymore. The sales landscape morphed dramatically—and so, too, did my thinking.

Buyers once had one job: to make the decision to buy from you. Today they wear a rack full of hats. They've become researchers and interviewers. They conduct product comparison studies. They compare buying experiences with those of others. All of this means many more voices—and an abundance of discrete perspectives—shape every buying decision.

Understanding this shift is crucial whether you're an ambitious novice salesperson, a seasoned team leader, or the head of an organization. Everyone must embrace a new mindset to come out on top in today's marketplace. For example, today's sales stars know how to reach each of multiple generations of buyers and to tap into their unique insights, buying habits, and priorities. This may not come naturally—people often struggle to relate to those from different generations and, in many settings, may not be inclined to try. As sellers we don't enjoy the luxury to pick and choose based on what feels comfortable and familiar; we must understand everyone in the client's buying community, uncover their unique motivation, curate all information to which we have access, and distill key messages into a few bullet points that can resonate with all.

To do this efficiently, you must cast aside the antiquated notion of an "ideal buyer." Instead recognize the need to understand and influence multiple buying personas in your market that have organized themselves into an unofficial "community." Not all are positioned to buy from you but make no mistake: each influences the decision-making of others who write the checks. I like how Lori Wizdo, Vice President and Principal Analyst at Forrester, sums it up: "For the B2B buying process, there is typically no single buyer. It's a team— therefore, individual personas aren't as important. There is no 'average' buyer. In fact, individual personas are almost irrelevant for B2B marketing. What you need to do is profile the buying team as a whole, based upon your own assessment of the buying team's journey."[15]

15   Michael Gerard, "The Buyer's Journey Demystified by Forrester," *Curata*, accessed January 23, 2019, http://www.curata.com/blog/the-buyers-journey-demystified-by-forrester/.

The Catch: Everyone Wants to Be Ideal and Unique

This shift presents something of a Catch-22 for salespeople and leaders: with the "ideal buyer" now a relic of a past age, we must treat *all* buyers as both ideal and unique. We must fashion specialized solutions that demonstrate why we represent the best fit for each customer's needs. Adopting such a personalized touch leads to real and measurable traction: 96 percent of decision makers say they'll consider a brand if the seller demonstrates a clear understanding of their business needs.[16] On the flip side, 77 percent will dismiss a seller who failed to do enough homework on company-specific business issues.

Sellers who burrow into the finer details often unearth a single critical issue that inevitably affects multiple parties, all of whom have skin in the game in finding a solution. So, when you're getting your arms around a customer's problem, be sure to reach out to each of these sources. Doing so may well mean the difference between a lost sale and a slam dunk.

I could quote a library's worth of studies showing how multiple buyers and influencers now sway every buying decision. But to keep things simple, consider the real-world insight shared by Wilhelmsen Ship Services, a Taiwan client: "Inside every organization, there are buyers, influencers and spies."

How many people compose this circle of multiple buyers? The precise number is unimportant; what matters is understanding it's never a party of one. **Getting in front of multiple points of contact, and building your buying community, is the only way you**

---

16 "The State of Sales 2018," LinkedIn, accessed January 6, 2019, https://business. linkedin.com/sales-solutions/b2b-sales-strategy-guides/the-state-of-sales-2018.

can paint a complete picture of problems you may help solve. It also helps you take full advantage of this compressed buying cycle. Within a shortened timeframe, we can gather better information from a broader field of people and thus close deals faster.

An industrial chemical distributor with whom I work is reaping huge benefits from adopting this personalized, multilayered approach. One of their biggest customers was a very large manufacturing buyer who manufactured a part for brakes on truck fleets. One day while standing in the client's lobby—trying to get a meeting with his traditional contacts in operations and maintenance—one seller overheard a conversation between a customer service representative and a salesperson. "I'm very concerned," one said to the other. "We're about to lose our biggest customer because of this manufacturing problem."

My savvy seller recognized information he could use. He rushed back to his office and contacted both parties from that conversation. He didn't say, "Hey, I eavesdropped," but he did use what he'd overheard to frame his approach. He shared concrete examples of how his product could help solve production problems plaguing both customer service and sales. He tweaked his message to speak to each contact's interests and needs. This was a Hail Mary pass, to be frank—but it worked. He closed the deal because he embraced fresh and more personal ways to express his value to members of the organization outside his traditional contacts.

I'm not suggesting you creep around prospects' hallways or root through their trash in efforts to happen upon the inside scoop. A fine line separates a smart seller from a stalker type. I *am* suggesting, however, that you embrace the power of personalization, recognize many people contribute to every decision today, and adjust your tactics accordingly.

Getting Right on the Money: Quick Tip

Try this exercise to expand your network of contacts inside every opportunity:

1. List all the ways you provide value to your client. More specifically, what problems do you solve and how does a client benefit from your work?
2. Next ask yourself, *Who else cares?* Brainstorm all other departments, outside of your main buyer, who should care about this value. For example, the client I just described would say they improve the manufacturing process, in turn helping produce more consistent products. Who else might care about this benefit? Members of the sales, customer service, finance, and marketing teams?
3. Develop persuasive messages you can share and questions you might ask of each potential influencer that will highlight your unique value. This might sound like, "Sales VPs love working with us because we help our clients churn out more consistent, high-quality products. This reduces product returns and reinforces customer loyalty. Does your team grapple with these issues?"

Expansion Questions at Work

Orbitform—an expert in fastening, forming and assembly solutions—also reaped rewards from identifying and engaging multiple players. Most of their salespeople are technical specialists who follow a very technical, manufacturing-focused track. In the past, they asked buyers what they needed and then provided it. They were far more focused on completing projects than on recognizing other issues and problems, which often meant missing golden opportunities. Their win percentages were lower than industry average and business development costs well above. Careful analysis revealed they were not engaging enough influencers and buyers in the sales cycle. During weekly training events, sales VP Bryan Wright urged sellers to ask expansive, open-ended questions to encourage in-depth dialogue. Soon, sellers posed probing queries like, "Who else is affected by this issue and how?" They began to wrap their arms around the full scope of each client's hurdles. They were able to bring others to the table affected by that same issue, which in turn uncovered new, related challenges. Ongoing coaching ultimately accelerated the sales process and improved closing rates, which led to higher sales and revenues and business development effectiveness that now runs much better than industry average You can do the same. When a buyer shares a problem they face, ask expansion questions:

- How does this affect others in your organization?
- Is your legal team troubled about the liability associated with this problem?
- What does this mean for your sales/operations/finance/ other teams?
- How does this challenge impact customer service?
- Do operators also have a sense of this issue?

- Does marketing care about fixing this problem?
- Is anyone else affected?

I call this building multithreaded value, because the answers you receive translate into additional insights and additional relationships. They also point you toward new conversations that will align the value you offer in products or services with the needs of each group affected. When this is complete, you will have a well-rounded, or multithreaded, presentation to share that increases your value to—and ROI for—the entire customer.

Before you apply these solutions, you must also bid adieu to another major assumption no longer relevant in today's marketplace: that selling is still about creating *partnerships* with your customer. Let's dig into this.

Buyers Value Insiders, Not Partners

We've been singing the praises of building "partnerships" with customers since the 1990s, which began with buyers clamoring for customized, scalable solutions. Sellers scrambled to draw buyers more closely into the sales process. For a time, it worked. But here's today's hard truth: your customers no longer want to partner with you; in fact, they *hate* partnering with you. It's nothing personal. They just despise the word and what it signals.

Why? Because when you're partners, you're outsiders, external players that must be managed. Trust needs to be earned and re-earned on both sides. Despite this detached reality, many sellers still treat buyers like "partners"; they practically label their customers as outsiders and therefore *become* one.

Stop thinking like an outsider; your customers want to work with an *insider*. They want you to know just as much about their business as they do. This granular knowledge empowers you to add real value to their operation and to bring it quickly. To reinforce personalized solutions that hinge on answers to probing questions, you must also establish and reinforce multiple touch points within your customer's organization. You must tailor your messages to those individuals to be like the smart seller with sharp ears in our earlier example.

Quality relationships are key, but don't neglect the *quantity* of connections. You can't be an insider until, as they said on the TV show *Cheers*, "everybody knows your name." Who is your primary contact? Who holds down the fort when your number one is away? Who is your contact's boss? Are all of those on either side of your main contact using your product or affected by your solution? Could or should they be? The more connections you establish and nurture within each organization, the more vital context you gain, and you get quicker responses and faster invitations to put your solution in front of buyers. I've yet to see an account lost due to a seller having *too many* connections, but I've seen millions left on the table as a consequence of having *too few*.

Flipping the script, consider that buyers may also desire multiple contacts inside *your* organization so they can get the help they need when they need it. The moldy concept of "owning" a particular relationship based on only one direct line of contact has vanished. Each person on your team now provides a distinct entry point into an organization, which in turn opens more channels to sell. Besides, if you fall sick or find yourself fortunate enough to summer in Tuscany this year, buyers will feel comforted that someone else has their back. With multiple contacts in your organization, it's much harder for customers to leave. Why? Your connection no longer depends on a single relationship; instead, both companies become intertwined, creating and reinforcing much stronger ties. **You retain and grow clients by developing more relationships, not by hoarding just a few.**

Engage Selling clients who are Right on the Money embrace what I call "insider selling." They encourage tight collaboration between all departments that interact with customers. By putting the customer experience first, sellers act much like orchestra conductors, choreographing relationships between various customer contacts and their own internal colleagues in management, customer service, installation, accounts receivable, and operations.

One is the most dangerous number in sales. If you're one person trying to stay atop multiple client relationships, you're almost certain to make costly mistakes. You're handcuffed. You cannot be proactive and initiate meetings to address client needs. You're forced to be reactive—constantly putting out fires, racing to address existing issues, and juggling countless calls for every question. While it's always nice as the seller to feel like the center of your client's attention, being so constrained limits your ability both to retain the client and to grow the business. Never let your ego jump in the way of being Right on the Money.

The chart below demonstrates the importance of creating multiple contacts on both sides of the table:

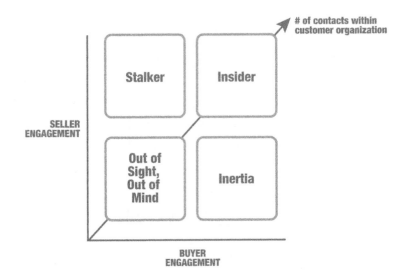

If you're a lone-wolf seller nurturing a single relationship inside your client account, you cannot maximize your relationship, because you too often fall **out of sight and out of mind**; you lack the presence to garner significant recognition.

This very thing happened to a client in Florida: they lost not one—but *two*—big accounts as a result of unforeseen internal changes within each customer's organization. In both cases they believed their position as top supplier was safe: they sold directly to the owner of one company and to the president of the other. But when the owner retired and the president quit, my client suddenly found itself on the outside, with no allies in either organization. This proved a painfully expensive lesson.

Just as dangerous—and even more common—is *inertia*: standing still when you need to keep moving. One sales leader with whom I work sold products to a large automotive company. For ten years he worked directly with one department. He developed such strong relationships with many in that department that the company had become one of the seller's biggest clients. Both parties were thrilled.

Alas, an organizational shift revealed something no one on the seller's team had realized: there were three more decision makers in different departments with whom they could have been connecting and selling. The seller's complacency—focusing on a single department and settling for just one large piece of business—meant missing out on $200,000 in added business for each of the last ten years. That's $2 million. Ponder that for a moment.

In sales, standing still is as wise as floating solo in the middle of the Pacific: you can count on a better-than-good chance of winding up dead in the water! And yet this happens all the time: sellers grow comfortable working with those they know will return their calls. Broadening this scope makes them uneasy, so they simply opt not to do it. To avoid this fate, think about where you could look for more connections and reflect on what you're potentially missing out on by allowing inertia to afflict your work.

Of course, there's an equally destructive flip side to inertia. When a handful of your team members hover over one buyer, you're not an insider: you're a *stalker*! As a result, you lack the bandwidth to see or leverage broader opportunities within the organization.

Now look at what happens when you avoid these mistakes and instead foster **multiple contacts between the client organization and yours. You become an *insider*.** You create an emotional barrier to change, and as a result the conversation transforms. Rather than clinging to your customer, begging them not to leave, the situation flips to your advantage: now they'll fight to keep *your* business.

Imagine You're Building a Spyder Bike on Steroids

To become an insider, you need to increase your bench strength, and that means creating connections both wide and deep. You need to marry the speed and aerodynamics of a motorcycle with the trusty steadiness of a solid four-door sedan. In other words, imagine you're building the sales equivalent of a three-wheeled Spyder Bike on steroids. It's all about threes. Find three contacts across three different divisions at three different managerial levels. And don't stop there: engage others within your organization in the process. Ask your marketing team to craft value statements and pitches for each of those nine people. Perhaps customer service can document and add to a database potential contacts from each category. Ask your delivery drivers, installation specialists, and project managers to help grow the list by sharing contacts. This allows you to infiltrate the organization from every conceivable angle.

Parman Energy Group recently identified a need to strengthen relationships with their biggest accounts. To this end the CEO requested a meeting with his counterpart at the buyer. He shared that he and the COO would be in the area and asked if he could spare half an hour for a quick sit-down, simply because they'd never met, and they were grateful for his business.

To their surprise the CEO gave them not thirty minutes but *two hours*! They began chatting about future business plans and ideas for growth. Over this time they cultivated a bond. Now those executives know they can always call on each other, and my client can be almost sure of ongoing transactions. This became a win-win they never would have uncovered had they not made the effort to increase and reinforce their connections.

The following is a tool we developed to help clients identify all their buying influencers. Company contacts are listed on the left, while buying contacts span the top. We built it as a simple Excel worksheet, but one could easily replicate it in any CRM. This structure helps identify gaps where more connections are required—the greater the white space, the more dangerous a position in which you find yourself.

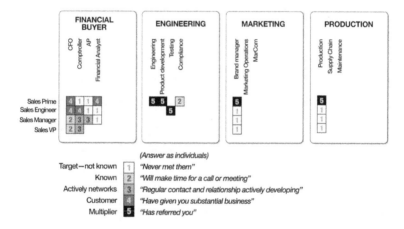

Become a Visionary

You must assemble a comprehensive snapshot of all people in your client's buying community. This includes not only identifying the players but deeply understanding their issues and cultivating multiple relationships between their organization and yours. Once you have done all this—and *only* then—you can persuasively demonstrate why you represent the best possible fit. Here your homework comes together. **Everyone and every-**

thing you know informs the development of a meaningful solution that addresses your buyer's every need. That's a vision, not just a pitch. Here's what this looks like in action:

For several years one client had pitched their product to a large sawmilling firm, but they could never unseat the competition. This changed suddenly when the incumbent supplier screwed up. An error forced the sawmill to go offline—they couldn't produce lumber their customers needed, and this downtime cost them $1 million in lost production. Even worse, the current supplier would be unable to fix the problem for two more days, which would have cost the sawmill another million dollars in lost revenue.

This misstep became my client's *in*. With a clear grasp of the problem at hand and with solid ideas about how to fix it, they swooped in and saved the day: within an hour they got the sawmill up and running, thus helping their new customer avoid more lost revenue. My client could later use this example as a potent case study with a robust value proposition: they could solve crises that others couldn't. What's more, the sawmill's leadership team came away so happy with my client's work that they began to tell others. Now my client uses multiple quantifiable and tangible value statements to win even more business.

In this sense, every customer can—and should—become a marketing tool to attract new customers. Customers want proof of how your work can help them. Case studies and testimonials resonate so well because they make prospective customers characters in the story, able to see themselves in this buying journey and more likely to award the sale. This is how you bring a vision to life.

ISAOSA, a client of mine in the Mexican agriculture business, did just that. They took a simple value proposition and broadened it upward and outward. They showcased their buyer's story and defined the solid value good relationships can provide.

ISAOSA had been working with a well-known sugar cane farmer in Mexico farmer who was celebrating extraordinary results and who frequently expressed his happiness in doing business with them. My client realized this customer could become a powerful evangelist for their brand. The farmer's willingness to share his story of a vision fully realized, combined with his status in the community, would open many doors. Still, they recognized no one but this particular farmer could tell this story so persuasively, so they flew, at their own expense, the primary contact, suppliers a few sales reps, and the president of the company to Brazil for meetings, plant tours, and round table discussions with other prospects. At each event the farmer raved about his experience, bringing to vivid life my client's vision for both current customers and prospects. They could also shore up that Spyder Bike three-by-three approach, as the ISAOSA team met new prospects, interacted with new contacts inside existing accounts, and ultimately secured new business. This modern, proactive approach helps my client win business in every major center they serve.

When crafting your vision, keep in mind your value proposition must *speak to the customer*. A prospect anxious about production and profit loss likely won't see themselves in a story centered on customer relationships; this would be like speaking German to one who only speaks English. Restating it louder and slower won't work either. **The only value that matters is the value that matters *to the buyer*.** That's why it's essential for multiple value statements to address different needs.

Here are some other strategies to help you craft clear, impactful visions:

- **Don't skimp on details.** We once taught sellers not to give away too much out of a worry free "consulting" might inspire buyers to just do it themselves. But with so little time on their hands, buyers need to know in advance how you can help. Companies that are Right on the Money understand that when potential buyers research on their own, they must be able to find a compelling reason to reach out. To facilitate this, sellers detail the unique business problems their customers have resolved thanks to their support. For example, when a technology client started flooding the market with detailed how-to videos describing problems and solutions and interviewing clients directly, they improved closing ratios and started growing faster than the market. Don't be worried about giving away your "secret sauce." You need to create an environment where prospects say: "I've learned so much for free, just imagine how much I'll pick up when I start *paying!*"

- **Align on sales value.** We often define sales value as the amount of money we'll receive when we sell something, but we must also show *meaningful monetization* behind that money. Define what those numbers represent in a way that matters to your buyer. Successful companies illustrate problems and solutions with both tangible and intangible value: along with the self-evident facts, they highlight the indirect, emotional, or peripheral benefits that differentiate them.

- **Apply insights internally.** You must get your employees on board before your clients can get there. That means all your people must become vocal evangelists for the value you bring. Your best people—and especially Millennials and Generation Z—stay longer, work harder, and prove more productive when they appreciate the value they create. Your results demonstrate this value, so make sure you also share those case studies and testimonials with your internal audiences.

Think Like a Competitor

Once you have mastered your new value statements and thought about how to leverage them to find new contacts inside each opportunity, it's time to do a deep dive into every account and opportunity to ensure you've left no stone unturned.

Whether you're spinning your wheels at the moment or hunting for new angles to secure new business, you can gain real value if you tackle a problem from a different perspective: that of your toughest competition. I call this "black-ops thinking," as it is much like the covert military strategies from which the name is borrowed. Gather a group of sellers and instruct them to think like a competitor. Ask the following questions:

- What is your current approach?

- What would you do differently?
- Who would you call?
- What problems do each of these people likely have?
- What unaddressed issues could the client be having?
- Who is the least obvious person to whom we could reach out?

Coming up with a comprehensive list of answers in your own head can be a real challenge, because you're only one person with a limited number of perspectives (often just one). Large consulting firms like McKinsey & Company have proved that multiple brains work better than one when chasing the best solution to a single problem.[17] That's why you must open up your dialogue. Grab four or five colleagues and present your client situation. Entertain all suggestions and solutions—don't write anything off as a bad idea. Multiple minds often uncover fresh approaches to new buyers and shape success stories and value propositions different from what you've tried in the past. To discover how one client, Parman Energy, has put this into practice visit www.rotm.me for a video interview.

Keep in mind, though, that sculpting these visions represents just one piece of the puzzle. You must also bring it all together: understand the buying community at large and the problems each contact could experience, and then align your solutions to illuminate a vision of success. Consider the following:

---

17   Ethan M. Rasiel, *The McKinsey Way: Using the Techniques of the World's Top Strategic Consultants to Help You and Your Business* (New York: McGraw-Hill, 1999).

1. If you know your buying community and have created a value proposition, but you fail to understand the
   issues your client is facing—and thus haven't aligned
   those visions to your client's specific needs—you're
   irrelevant.

2. If you know your buying community and the problems
   your client faces, but you lack any visionary solutions to
   share, you are useless.

3. If you know the problems the buyer community faces
   and have visionary solutions to share, but you have no
   client connection, you're a secret—hidden from those
   who need you most.

The good news: if you have all three, you've got the inside scoop and the buyer's complete attention, and you leave no room for the competition to sneak in a side door. You're Right on the Money.

So far we've explored at length your customer-centric approach to being Right on the Money. All of this involves an external focus. You gain solid insights into today's evolving sales landscape and can fashion a sound strategy to execute properly in this brave new world of selling. However, as we saw in the illustration near the end of chapter 1, this is just one half of the Right on the Money equation. The second half is about understanding and implementing an important new concept—*Sales Velocity*.

It's time to harness this and apply it to yourself and your sales team. Let's get started.

Chapter 6

SALES VELOCITY

Imagine this scenario:

You're driving along a highway. Everything in your car seems in flawless working order—except for the speedometer, the needle of which doesn't budge. Only at stoplights do you have any clue how fast or how slow you're moving. All you can venture are best guesses about your speed based on highway signs, towns falling into your rear view, and any other hints you catch as you zip by.

Sure, you'll pull up at your destination eventually, but you can't be sure precisely when. Might you do something to arrive sooner? Do you tempt fate each time you pass a police cruiser at the roadside? You just don't know. One thing is for certain, though: by the time you arrive, you'll be the world's biggest fan of having a functioning speedometer in your car.

Think of Sales Velocity as an instrument panel for your business, your best set of tools to answer the crucial question: ***How*** *fast is my team making sales and earning revenue?*

Alas, just as with speedometers, few think much about Sales Velocity until it falls conspicuously absent. People don't fully understand its power as a decision-making tool. That's a big mistake. Let's fix it now.

What Is Sales Velocity and Why Is It So Important?

To be Right on the Money, it's vital to stay focused on performance metrics, because this data reveals how well your efforts are converting directly into sales and provides powerful insights into your unique circumstances. Sales Velocity quickly becomes one of your most important metrics—and predictors—of success. And, fortunately, it's very easy to calculate.

Too often people assume that solutions to complex problems demand equally complicated questions and an exhaustive list of inputs. In reality, determining Sales Velocity requires only that you ask a simple set of purposeful questions. You measure four selling-based activities:

1. the number of **opportunities** in your sales pipeline;
2. the average **deal size** your team achieves, measured in dollar value;
3. your **win/lose rate**, expressed as a percentage of new business successfully closed; and
4. your team's **sales cycle** time from prospect to close, measured in days.

Sales Velocity Makes You Think Like a Data Scientist

Selling is emotional, yet the metrics behind sales performance center purely on cold, hard facts. That's why Sales Velocity is so accurately predictive. It's also why I argue that top sellers and sales leaders think like *data scientists.* They let numbers inform their decision-making, including where to improve and why.

Once you capture numbers for the four activities listed, you possess the raw data to start making sense of your Sales Velocity using the following formula:

To excel, you must track Sales Velocity over time and benchmark your numbers against those of other teams or individuals. Not only does this arm you to compare effectiveness of individual reps or regions, it also reveals how incremental changes to sales processes can affect your business—for better or worse. Why? Addressing any of these activities alters how readily you close sales and earn revenue and thus changes your results. After all, Sales Velocity measures how much money you're pulling in daily. Armed with this knowledge, your understanding of your unique sales problem begins to evolve, and stronger solutions emerge.

Once you deepen your understanding of the four components of the formula—and the relationships between them—you can forecast with tighter precision and optimize your sales process for faster sales and higher conversion rates.

For example, a rep in a new territory can easily boost Sales Velocity by growing the number of opportunities in the pipeline; in a new environment, abundant new opportunities are up for grabs. By contrast, a sales rep working a more established territory can heighten velocity by trimming cycle time or increasing average deal size.

Using your formula, you can hone in on more specific numbers in pursuit of performance improvements of up to 25 percent. Here's an example:

Let's say you're pursuing thirty opportunities with an average deal size of $10,000, a win rate of 0.37, and a cycle time of ninety days. This calculates out to a Sales Velocity of $1,233. Were you to increase deal size to $11,000 and pare cycle time to eighty-one days, your Sales Velocity would jump to $1,507, a 25-percent boost in average daily sales volume.

Improving Your Velocity One Metric at a Time

Now that you understand just how much these variables can transform your bottom line, let's take a closer look at how changes in each can increase or decrease Sales Velocity.

Increasing the Number of Opportunities

Before you do anything else, you must fully define the opportunity problem you're looking to solve. This will help you craft your strategy to increase opportunities.

Look carefully at your current pipeline. Are you falling behind in hitting goals, or are you on track and positioned to accelerate sales? If the former, you must focus on pipeline development; if the latter, you need to bulk up an already healthy pipeline.

Once you gain a handle on your challenges, you can better fashion winning solutions. What goals, once met, would solve your issue and propel your business to new heights? Before you strategize that next move and set goals, pause for a moment, and reflect on the nuances within the big picture from start to finish.

Setting goals only works if targets are achievable and strike an appropriate balance between quality and quantity. For most of my clients, a targeted 10- to 20-percent increase in opportunities generates a solid batch of new leads. However, you must separate the gunk and sludge from silver and gold in the planning stage—not when you're deep into a campaign. There's no point in amassing an imposing list of unchecked new prospects if each of the leads is terrible. If you do, you'll dig yourself an even deeper hole and drive away your best sellers in the process, because they'll grow frustrated with your lack of foresight. Plan first—then execute.

Winning tactics are never one-size-fits-all. Yours should be determined by those first two steps: defining your sales problem and determining sensible goals. Depending on the outcome of those exercises, you might pursue one or all of the following opportunity-boosting tactics:

- **Go back.** Within your existing pipeline, you almost certainly know customers you could ramp up to gold-status clients. After all, not all your previous wins look the same. With which clients can you craft new opportunities? Who has been buying less or more than in years past—and why? Which customers have undergone organizational changes that may have created a need for new products or services? Identify them, make contact, and sleuth out whether or not new opportunities await.

- **Get inside.** Internal referrals prove powerful and effective because they help you leapfrog buyer objections. Word-of-mouth internal referrals convey true, positive impressions no amount of advertising could buy. How do you get them? Ask! One technology client of mine focused on cold calls and struggled with opportunity creation. Three grueling hours on the phone each day scraped up only two qualified opportunities. When she shifted to a referral strategy and began asking each buyer to introduce her to a new division or department, she started to generate three new opportunities *per hour*. That's more than a 300-percent increase!

- **Go outside.** Similar in effectiveness to internal referrals, external recommendations lead to the highest closing rate in sales today. Ask your best customers for referrals to others like them, including suppliers, partners, customers of their own, or even people they know through networking.

- **Get "unlost."** Working from your pipeline, revisit near misses, lost sales, and dormant accounts; you'll find missed opportunities in there. Donald LeBlanc did this and exploded $900,000 in sales into $3 million in just one year! He tripled his business simply by reaching out to people who *didn't* buy from him before, who became buyers after he brought a fresh and more compelling case to renewed discussions.

- **Get networking.** When you're prospecting nothing beats face-to-face interaction, but if that's not possible, you can also network online. All networking speeds up the decision-making and buying cycle because it personalizes your work. Find networking opportunities in your sales territory or in online associations, and start engaging with prospects in places meaningful to them—both virtual and in the real world. Remember ... draw on your Critical Mass Influence.

- **Go social.** You already know cold calls are as dead as video stores. Social media and referrals have become the essential go-to tool to preheat calls with strangers and lay the groundwork for relationships before you pick up the phone. It's how you grow a *network* of like-minded people: using the most effective medium to *engage* with them so they want to connect with you. You start participating in meaningful conversations about topics buyers care about, thus creating the ideal conditions to convert prospects into loyal buyers. Remember, this can be easily done with the Triad Tempo we discussed in chapter 4.

Increasing Your Average Opportunity Size

If your goal is to boost average opportunity size, you must *stop* doing the following during the planning stage:

- **Chasing opportunities that are too small.** To land bigger deals, start by defining the kind of opportunity you need to pursue, and measure that against the opportunities you are pursuing and closing. Your ideal opportunities today may be different than those pictured previously, so you may need to push yourself out of your comfort zone. Your job is to not pursue everything that comes your way. Your job is to pursue those best opportunities that help you exceed your goal while being profitable for you and your company.

- **Expecting the solution to come to you all at once.** Be incremental in your planning. Set realistic expectations both for your business and for your target customer. One client of mine refocused its sales strategy to boost average opportunity size. They correctly determined they would fall well short of their desired 50-percent growth goal for a single year. Setting instead a target of 15 percent, and raising the bar as they progressed, generated the momentum and confidence necessary to grow.

- **Guessing.** All effective plans to augment opportunity size are methodical and driven by hard facts and data that together shape a compelling story. Start tracking your efforts and measuring their impact. Gather needed data using your in-house financial system, a CRM, or even a spreadsheet. Your KPIs must show short-term, medium-term, and long-term progress toward your goal.

With your planning completed, let's unpack what it looks like to execute an opportunity-boosting strategy to increase Sales Velocity.

- **Look inward.** Always start by selling more to existing customers—that's your inside track. Selling more to customers with whom you have a history is always faster and more profitable than chasing after new customers. Working beyond that base, prioritize customers that present the biggest opportunities to increase average deal size by looking at how many locations they maintain, whether they are international or local, and the size of their employee populations. Sure, it may take much longer to reel in larger companies, but they always provide better opportunities for long-term growth.

- **Be ruthless.** This is a necessary step, but I won't kid you: it's tough. All top-performing sales leaders regularly conduct a cutthroat review of existing opportunities. They zero in on those dragging down their average deal size and cut them loose or jettison them to inside sales. Zach Sutton at Hunt and Sons in Northern California routinely steers his sellers away from opportunities "not worth chasing" because they are too small for both the seller and the company to make a profit. He's right—and he's smart. At the date of publishing, his team was the only one in his region hitting their targets.

- **Aim high.** Ask any skilled negotiator, and they'll tell you the art of deal-making involves being skilled at setting goals higher than necessary. Remember, though, you can only do this *after* you have planned successfully and targeted the right customers; as I shared earlier, your stretch targets must ultimately be *realistic*. Aim *past* your targeted deal size, never at it. Build in a bonus buffer; you'll be surprised how often that works in your favor.

- **Look elsewhere.** If you sell to a client whose territory comprises only one or two regions, find similar clients whose scope is national or international. This means getting comfortable talking to high-level buyers. One client successfully boosted their average deal size from $10,000 to $50,000 by mastering the rapport skills needed to make a compelling case to VP-level clients.

- **Coach regularly.** Invest in coaching and skill development for yourself and your team. This ensures none fall into the trap of chasing the wrong client or picking a targeted deal size out of sync with your organization's goals.

Improving Your Closing Ratio

Closing ratios are next up in our formula. Here you concentrate on your win/lose rate; this is all about *execution*. But to close—and thus execute—effectively, you must uncover important facts as you qualify potential buyers early in your sales cycle. You must understand *why* each customer is buying from you by securing the following answers:

- Based on what buying criteria will a buyer choose you over your competitors?
- What issue or goal is the buyer counting on your product or service to improve or solve?
- What's the buyer's desired ROI? What value do they ascribe to your product or service?

How do you uncover these answers? Use three key tactics:

1. **Create a sense of urgency by monetizing the problem.**
   Your job is to stimulate a sense of urgency in your client's mind that they'll achieve a desired return on investment by choosing your product or service. You do that during the qualification stage by monetizing your customer's problem. The more successful you are at this, the better your closing ratio will be.

   When I sold software to companies in the resources sector, I used this tactic often. For one customer we understood a bushel of money was up for grabs if we could help them make better decisions, and in less time, around the drilling of new oil wells. They sought to increase the number of wells they drilled (and pumped from) each year; we knew the dollars associated with this improvement were far greater than the price tag for the service we were promoting. But they only understood the potential ROI because I'd invested real time asking probing questions about their operations, including time-to-drill and the annual value of each well. In doing so, I demonstrated in clear, financial terms the value of those extra wells.

   Today time-saving strategies can help you showcase your importance with fewer hours logged. Three clients of mine in vastly different industries—software, fertilizers, and industrial lubricants—have each developed an online ROI calculator that demonstrates to customers how much they can use, produce, or save by choosing my clients' products. This structured approach has ballooned closing ratios from about 30 percent to 40 percent because my clients no longer focus on price per unit and instead home in on ROI for the program.

2. **Connect with the right people in multiples.**
We've established that your account penetration is never complete with a single contact, because multiple influencers, advisors, and buyers influence and participate in the buying process, no matter the size of the organization. The more people with whom you engage inside your account, the more likely you are to close, simply because you navigate a more complete road map of buying criteria and priorities.

This is not to say you should focus solely on boosting the quantity of contacts with no regard to quality. You must evolve high-quality relationships with as many people as possible. You must sell high, wide, and deep for two reasons. First to gain a broad range of discrete perspectives. Not all will share the same point of view as to the problem they seek to solve with your product or service. For instance, your contacts in finance may see things quite differently than customer service. Both viewpoints are valid and need to be considered in your solution.

The second reason you broaden contacts is to ensure your network includes everyone with decision-making authority. It's not enough to find people who *like* what you're selling. I learned a hard lesson years ago when selling to the US Air Force. I visited all major command groups and obtained their buy-in on my solution. When I went to the Pentagon, ostensibly to tie a bow on my deal, I was stopped in my tracks by a high-ranking general who looked over all my work and barked, "While it's nice all those people are on board, Colleen, the last time I checked, they all report to me!" It all boils down to this: you will hear "Yes!" more often if you connect with those with authority to give you the green light.

3. **Sell to referrals.**

   Our research at Engage Selling shows that while a cold lead might hope for a one-in-twenty-five chance of closing, a referred lead boosts this average to *one in two*. This is a huge improvement—but it hinges on first establishing a strong referral program. Granted, not everyone boasts a client base that can yet support many referrals. Some of you are entering new markets or launching products and services. Don't despair if this situation applies to you—your focus will center on the first two tactics I've outlined in this section.

   The rest of you should ask for referrals—*every day*. Look for introductions to external partners, customers, and suppliers. Seek an audience with internal colleagues in adjacent business units, locations, or departments. The more you ask, the more you'll receive and the faster your closing rate will take off.

Reducing the Time It Takes to Close Opportunities

The final step in our formula involves shrinking your individual sales-cycle length from prospect to close. This is the most critical denominator in the Sales Velocity formula, and it influences everything else you do. The faster you close more business, the sooner you'll meet and exceed revenue targets.

With this in mind, let's look at three must-do tactics that will lead to positive, lasting improvements in your sales-cycle speed.

1. **Seed the market well.**

   Our research consistently shows that customers across all markets respond enthusiastically to timely, meaningful information that helps them make better buying decisions. That's why you must "seed the market" by implementing your Triad Tempo online by posting and sharing high-value, practical, and timely content. Doing so makes you known to a potential buyer and thus converts a cold lead into an almost warm one. You bypass the getting-to-know-you stage and start building a relationship from your first interaction—and on a foundation of trust, since you've already provided something of value.

   One client initiated a proactive email campaign featuring case studies, prospect sheets, and ROI statements. This outreach moved valuable information in front of a broad range of potential buyers and ultimately ramped up the speed with which the sales team could close new business.

2. **Respond like clockwork.**

   When you set a timer on your wristwatch or your phone, you bring discipline to your personal task list. Use the same thinking to nudge your sales team to respond like clockwork to new inbound leads. A recent InsideSales.

com study found that up to 75 percent of all new sales land with the seller who responds first to an inbound lead. In today's marketplace your customer reaches out when she's ready to buy—not before. And when she's ready, you have *one* shot to be first, so don't blow it!

To ensure an urgent-yet-calculated response to potential new business, one client implemented a service agreement between their sales and marketing groups to respond to all leads within an hour. In short order the time leads took to close reduced by 40 percent. If you're concerned such a dramatic demand will be met with more resistance than unbridled enthusiasm, adopt an incremental approach. Start by mandating a response within one business day, and after a week pare down this expectation to four hours. Measure and continue to shrink the window as your team makes progress.

Another proven technique is to block time daily for your sellers to stay on top of follow-up calls. As James Clear points out in his excellent book *Atomic Habits: An Easy & Proven Way to Build Good Habits & Break Bad Ones*: "You do not rise to the level of your goals. You fall to the level of your systems."[18] Be unfailingly systematic. Set a recurring appointment in your calendar to ensure no one books a meeting during that time. Include buffer times between meetings to squeeze in one or two calls or to handle incoming emails. This way, you'll never fall behind.

---

18   James Clear, *Atomic Habits: An Easy & Proven Way to Build Good Habits & Break Bad Ones* (New York: Avery, 2018).

3. **Ask for the sale.**

   You'd think this would be obvious; it's not. In all my years of coaching salespeople, the biggest and most consistent mistake I witness is that sellers don't formally ask the customer for the sale. You must integrate the following question into every conversation with those considering your proposal: *Are you ready to move forward now?* Each time your team fails to ask, they squander an opportunity to close more business in less time. For more ways to ask for the sale, visit www.rotm.me.

   Just as important: be sure your sales team poses the closing question to someone with decision-making authority. Getting to "yes" means nothing unless you're dealing with someone who not only understands the value of your offering and the sense of urgency to make the purchase but who can also accelerate the sale.

Sales Velocity is a powerful metric every sales leader must know inside and out. It tasks you to assess the current state of your organization, map out a matrix of possible futures, and pave a road to greater success. And while Sales Velocity measures how rapidly you're making sales and earning revenue—and provides a spotlight on how to realize greater sales—it gifts you with something even more valuable. **You gain an understanding of the relationship between the four key activities that constitute your Sales Velocity: opportunities, deal size, closing rate, and sales-cycle speed.** With this critical knowledge, you position yourself to vastly improve outcomes, sell more in less time, and generate much greater revenue. If you want to calculate it for yourself, visit this book's website at www.rotm.me for the calculator and instructions.

Chapter 7

CORPORATE VELOCITY: BRINGING CHANGE INSIDE YOUR ORGANIZATION

e've talked about how sweeping, massive changes continue to reinvent our marketplace. We now need a new map of this radically transformed landscape. We must revisit how we sell, including how we think about and interact with prospective buyers well before any sale ever takes place.

In chapter 6 we explored in depth a critical concept each sales leader must embrace—Sales Velocity. The core idea is this: unless you know how fast you're moving—with cold, hard numbers to back you up—you cannot know where you're winning and where you're losing.

You need to apply this same outlook across your entire organization. The business must adapt to change, just as must the people within. Alas, unlike individuals, organizations pivot slowly. Long before there's any true realization of a need to shift direction, team leaders may become bogged down in faulty thinking. They assume any failure to achieve expected profitability rests squarely on the shoulders of their sales team. This is simply not true.

Don't be so quick to jump to conclusions: remember the earlier example of the installers whose bashing of the flimsy material and faulty screws inadvertently torpedoed millions in furniture sales?

To be clear, there's no question sellers falling short of targets remains a real problem. We've always known less than 60 percent of companies typically hit their targets each year—but now, coming out of the 2020 lockdown, 60 percent anticipate a *decrease* in their ability to hit quotas, with 18 percent expecting a significant decrease.[19] While we of course want salespeople to consistently hit targets regardless of the state of the market, it's a mistake to blame them solely should they come up short.

Think less like a judge and more like a diagnostician. Spend more time asking *why* profits are lower than you'd like, rather than obsessing over *who* to blame.

What you may find is that you have more of an issue generating revenue than shortcomings within your sales team. Consider this simple difference. Each time you generate a sale, you register a purchase order. This is, in essence, a contract with a customer that you'll deliver something. Generating *revenue*, though, means you actually hold that cash in

---

19 "The LinkedIn State of Sales Report 2020," January 2021, https://business. linkedin.com/sales-solutions/b2b-sales-strategy-guides/the-state-of-sales-2020-report.

hand. Sales and revenue may be interrelated, but this does not mean the latter hinges entirely on the former. Yes, you keep your sales team on the hook to bring in those purchase orders and to get contracts signed—but revenue generation is the job of the entire company.

In my work I'm often tasked with putting on my contractor hat. I'm brought in to fix what I'm assured is a "broken" sales team. More often than not, I end up fixing operational and process-driven glitches less about sales than about revenue at large.

Consider a manufacturing client that unexpectedly ended up 10 percent behind on targets. Sellers were doing their job; contracted sales were at plan. In spite of this, revenue was lagging. Why? Because invoices stated the company "reserved the right to ship up to 10 percent more or less than ordered," and the company had frequently been shipping *less.*

The sales team had no clue they were being sabotaged by a blind spot: the amount of product actually going out. Beyond a drop in revenue, this also led to late payments, because buyers were forced to reissue purchase orders. This also meant lost sales, since customers often wouldn't reorder after encountering trouble the first time around. What's more, the process was creating massive delays in collecting payments, as purchase order numbers and invoices needed to be corrected, which in turn translated into lumpy revenue. Based on numbers of contracts signed—the only part within the control of the sales team—the company was right on track. Had we not widened our lens and adopted a more holistic view of what was happening across all parts of the business, we may never have found—nor solved—the problem.

Do You Have a Sales *Prevention* Department?

Throughout your organization faulty operations can hinder profits, even if your sales team hits all targets. If other organizational issues stand in the way, addressing the sales team alone won't fix it. Consider just a few examples of how problems in other departments can drag down overall revenue:

1. **Treacherous technology snafus:** One high-tech client was so eager to ship a product that they didn't test their current software against an upcoming version of the platform's operating system. Everything crashed. It took months to fix the mistake, and during that time many customers defected.

2. **Painful production problems:** You can't sell what you can't produce. If you're not generating your product in consistently reliable quantities, you may be repeating the mistake made by one of my mining clients. The operations VP had shrunk production yields on one product, but sales targets remained unchanged at about 20 percent above the new production output. Because less product entered the marketplace, the sales team regularly sold out but still left the company well short of revenue goals.

3. **Faulty follow-up:** One engineering consulting firm discovered sales were dipping simply because teams were taking more than two weeks to issue quotes on projects. By the time they finally delivered these estimates, many customers had moved on. Similarly, a hardware company fell behind on its production schedule and began

missing important shipping deadlines. Again, customers weren't interested in waiting, so they defected.

4. **Customer-repellant IT policies:** Virtual selling is a must these days, and sellers must prove adaptable to meet the desires of their prospects. For example, they need free access to, and be expert on, all platforms their customer's request. While IT and legal need to find ways to do this safely and to prevent cyberattacks, an all-out ban of specific platforms, websites, appliances, and apps prevents sellers from doing their work effectively. For example, when an IT department forbids a seller from using a client-requested video platform, downloading an app, or using social media as a prospecting tool, the company handcuffs the seller and saddles her with a competitive disadvantage.

Do any of these circumstances sound familiar? If so, **you may find a *sales prevention department* growing right under your nose.** They pop up in the most unlikely places. For one *Fortune* 500 company with whom I work, their sales prevention department took root within their IT group. Here's their story:

One of the company's VPs of sales worked on a six-year-old laptop—ancient by today's standards. When it started to slow down, he called the IT department. "Can I have a new laptop?" he asked, explaining his machine just wasn't functioning as it once had.

"Sorry," they said. "Our policy states we can't give you a new laptop until your old one breaks. Call us then."

Sure enough, my client's laptop soon bought the farm. He took the corpse to IT. "Why are you using such an old laptop?" the technician asked. "Why didn't you come to us sooner?"

"I did," the VP replied, his patience waning. "And you told me not to contact you until it broke."

"Well, you should have *lied*." This was the unofficial answer: to *lie*. Worse, it took the IT department two weeks to obtain a new laptop and another week to get it in full working order. This key seller, responsible for hundreds of millions in revenue, endured several unproductive weeks because of this comedy of errors.

Sometimes toxic internal politics prove the culprit. With one client I found myself at ground zero in a pitched battle between two divisions of a single company as they jockeyed to secure a sale. The first division's general manager asked for pricing from the second. That division's GM refused to provide it because he insisted on "owning" the buyer. The bid went in without participation of the holdout division, resulting in the loss of a 2.8-million-unit sale.

Sadly, I can draw upon endless horror stories like these. The good news? You're not doomed to a similar fate—provided you mercilessly eliminate sales prevention departments. How? By demanding flawless execution throughout your organization—not just in sales.

Execute Flawlessly

Flawless execution demands frequent, clear, and practical communication and collaboration. You must run a perfectly organized house that hums along and continuously addresses the needs of buyers. The following solutions will help you overcome common roadblocks to sales and revenue generation, thus helping your team stay Right on the Money with every buyer who walks through the door.

Keep Your Sales Team Engaged

Although you must ultimately adopt a holistic approach to organizational management, it *is* important to start with sales. Among the most critical factors in ensuring that success continues after the buyer says "yes" is to ensure that the sales team stays engaged. Their job must continue beyond the moment they hold a contract in hand. Whether your salespeople know it or not, they maintain a vested interest beyond securing a customer's signature; they should also feel invested in making sure the rest of the operation runs smoothly. When they can spot problems—such as the insidious roots of an emerging sales prevention department—they can address pinch points and help find additional solutions quickly. The goal? To make sure your buyer *remains* yours.

Think back to our furniture installation team that kept driving away follow-up sales. Not until a seller spotted the behavior "live" did the company identify this particular pinch point. Because the seller stayed engaged after the deal was closed, he saw what was up. When he made the suggestion to retrain the installation team, the business finally began to take off.

One way to drive engagement is to pay sellers upon implementation, rather than at the time of sale. This encourages them to stay engaged—which is particularly vital, since the faster a client is onboarded and using your product, the more loyal they often become (more on this soon).

Be Careful about Your Customer Activation Process

Your customer activation structure is connected to your engagement strategy. It's become very popular for companies to maintain a customer activation structure involving multiple players. One person secures the sale, activates the buyer, and then transitions him or her over to an account or customer relationship manager before moving on to the next sale. **While it's fine for others to become go-to contacts, if this transition isn't made smoothly, you could be setting yourself up for reduced or even lost sales.**

Remember a buyer's trust is a delicate treasure. Every time they work with someone new, a seller must re-establish and reinforce such trust. The smallest misstep is sure to be exaggerated in the client's mind. If customers feel shuffled around, they won't be comfortable. In addition, a clunky handoff causes delays, hinders implementation, and prevents you from accelerating time to cash.

If your process involves a handoff, you're best to introduce the account or customer relationship management team early in the sales cycle—no later than in the presentation phase, when you first lay out expectations following the sale. The team to take over should attend the meeting and introduce themselves if possible. At the very least, show the buyer photos of each individual with whom they'll interact and offer a thorough description of the onboarding structure so your buyer knows what to expect. Otherwise, you risk leaving your client feeling like the victim of a bait and switch, which can erode both trust and profits. At Engage Selling our success with clients has led to a best practice everyone can use. Here's how it works:

We encourage our clients to come to meetings with the following diagram. It might be captured on a PowerPoint slide, printed on a sheet of paper, or even drawn right in front of the buyer. We tell them to ask a series of questions to craft what we call a *buying project plan.*

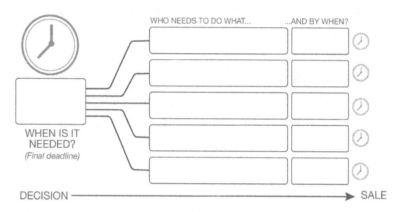

The first question determines *when* the buyer needs the product or service. Fleshing out the rest of the interim steps helps both buyer and seller know what must happen before the sale is truly complete and at what point each needs to occur to meet the ultimate target date. For example, the buyer may learn that contracts and vendor agreements must be signed and installation scheduled, all ahead of their target date. As such, buyer and seller must work together to meet all steps in a timely manner.

The seller never arrives with a prepopulated plan. Instead, the seller writes all details out as they discuss them with the buyer, so the customer can witness the plan developing in real time. As a result, no buyer feels he or she is being handed a prepackaged process. It's fully customized to each client's needs.

You can visit www.rotm.me to download sample scripts of how to put this into action.

As everything begins to gel and the buyer fully embraces the process, you facilitate introductions to all who may be involved in next steps. If training needs to be scheduled with a team member, or if an account manager must be assigned, this introduction is made then and there, so the buyer sees it as a natural part of implementation (and you avoid any sense of bait and switch). Ultimately, the buyer feels the seller has done this before, that they're safe and can feel confident in their hands, and that a solid plan will guide onboarding. This builds trust with everyone recruited to the project.

Always Have a Backup

I grow weary repeating this as often as I do, but here it is once more: your company MUST have a backup system in place—especially with key accounts. You always need another person within your group who knows your accounts inside and out. That way if a primary contact embarks on a monthlong Mediterranean cruise, comes down with a nasty virus (it happens), moves to a chalet overseas, or experiences any other event that changes directions, there's no loss of trust. Instead, you facilitate a seamless transfer to seller number two within your team. The same goes for employees in all other departments who interact with your buyer. People must have the knowledge and resources to take over if necessary—no exceptions.

What can go wrong if you fail to set up these stopgaps? You could ask a manufacturing client of mine. When their supply chain manager left on vacation for two weeks without any backup, no one knew new materials needed to be ordered to keep production on track. When that order failed to go through, it created a two-week delay that angered buyers and logjammed sales—after all, you can't sell what you can't produce.

Now consider what can happen with appropriate backups in place. A client in the aerospace industry knows only limited customers buy their product, but each is a huge account. The company can neither afford to let any buyers down nor afford to miss a single sale. So, every member of the inside sales team—the revenue generators—maintains a backup. Account managers introduce backups to the buyer and provide all necessary information for the buyer to reach each easily if necessary. Those backup staff members also attend regularly scheduled meetings and business reviews—just as an understudy shows up to a rehearsal for a play—so they know everything the primary does. With this solid system in place, the company never misses an order, buyers are seldom dissatisfied, and account managers can rest easy knowing they're covered should they ever become unavailable. The seamless experience pays off in a big way.

RelaDyne has taken this backup system one step further by partnering up sales managers in adjacent territories. Sales manager partners attend each other's meetings and coaching sessions so that they are aware of the basic selling environment and situation of that territory. They get to know the sellers on the team and the dynamic. This way when one manager is out sick or on vacation (or leaves the organization suddenly), the transfer of the management of the team to the backup is seamless.

Getting Right on the Money: Quick Tip

Ensuring clear communication and collaboration between any department in contact with your buyers is fundamental to preserving this seamless experience. Doing so entails creating service-level agreements between departments. Flawless execution demands this.

Take this advice from my client Mountz Torque with some examples of agreements you must establish:

- Marketing and Sales departments must agree on the speed with which sellers will respond to leads. If this doesn't happen—and you find Marketing running a program without Sales there to execute it—the process won't be effective.
- A service-level agreement must state that Marketing will generate a specific volume of leads and that Sales must accept or reject them within a set period—say twenty-four or forty-eight hours.
- Sales and Finance need a service-level agreement setting rules for order entry and credit approvals. Inside sales must also adhere to a service-level agreement with buyers on response times.

Connect Strategy and Execution

To be Right on the Money, your strategy and execution must align with your service-level agreements. One client realized this when they found themselves in over their heads as they attempted to expand their business. This Quebec-based company wanted to start selling in other provinces, so they hired a sales team to start knocking on doors. Unfortunately, they failed to plan for success after new sales were made! The sales team did their job well: they brought in boatloads of new buyers. But soon after the ink dried, my client realized they wouldn't be able to work these new buyers into their regular shipment line. They lacked the warehouses or trucks to meet the increased demand, which created significant downstream delays. As a result, they had to tell all buyers their shipments wouldn't arrive on time—not a great way to enter a new market!

The solution? **You must work downstream on every component of strategy and determine how it will affect each division and every buyer.** When you bring a new idea to the table, start by creating an execution plan. Here's what that might look like for a new sale to a new customer:

- Gather all players involved. Is there a customer service manager, an onboarding manager, a credit manager, and representatives from Operations, Shipping, and Delivery in the room?
- Assign relevant responsibilities to various team members and specify completion dates for each task.
- Schedule check-ins and make providing updates mandatory for all parties.
- Review the plan before you begin implementing—and course-correct as you go. To quote the smart sales managers at Sun Coast resources "Never let the team go in blind!"

While building your execution plan, create a customer-journey map to capture the post sale path your customer will take over the lifetime of your relationship. Start by naming every phase of the customer's journey with you. You might include things like onboarding, implementation, retention, growth, etc. Next list critical employees, department tools, and employees with whom the buyer will interact in that phase. With all touchpoints in place, reach out to your buyers and find out which are most critical.

Next seek out customer perspectives about what you do well and where you fall short. For instance, has the customer taken issue with your shipping procedures in the past? Plot those areas most critical and those that cause the most pain. Notice any trends? Does one item keep showing up in the upper-left quadrant? Using this matrix, you'll be more objective and better positioned to identify and fix those items most important to your customers.

Don't overcomplicate this process. The real problem is that most people overthink it—and when they do, nothing gets done. Keep it simple. Don't just *think* like a customer—*ask* your customers to do the thinking for you! Build their points into your map. With a clear pathway, you can smooth the rockiest sections first, thus making the journey as unobstructed as possible. Review and repeat this process quarterly to ensure you address any emerging priorities or issues.

Sales prevention departments and revenue fails happen when companies take their eyes off the buyer and focus only on internal goals. When this happens, follow-up often falls off too, which creates more space for errors and loss. Getting your house in order and fixing any issues that arise isn't difficult, but it does require methodical execution and focus to ensure you keep asking the right questions.

For everything you do, you must know how it affects the buyer experience and your ability to convert sales into cash. Therefore, do a thorough review of every part of your organization—not just Sales—to ensure everyone stays on the same page. Continue to map and refine the buyer's journey. With everything necessary in place—along with a system to address anything that isn't—you jump one step closer to meeting and exceeding your targets.

Corporate velocity reveals the changes you must realize within your organization. Follow this series of actionable strategies to ensure needed adjustments can take root within your team and within your every department. Once this is done, your next step is to clarify what needs measuring so you can track progress and course-correct where required. In the next chapter, we'll endeavor to jump over a hurdle with which many of today's sales leaders and organizations struggle: generating and using the right data.

Chapter 8

CONTROL YOUR DATA ...
BEFORE IT CONTROLS YOU

"**Y**ou can have data without information, but you cannot have information without data." This sage advice from Daniel Keys Moran, an American computer programmer and science fiction writer, can help refine your pursuit of a boost in sales. Ignore it at your peril.

Recently I worked with a B2B apparel company that employed three distinct sets of data in making sales forecasts. The product development group created one batch to forecast new product enhancements twenty-four months in advance, with 20 percent of sales targeted to come from those new products. The procurement team's data projected an eighteen-month outlook since they would need to order product from factories with time to spare to meet deadlines. And the sales team employed yet another forecast, tied to the fiscal year and based on growth targets inspired by the previous year's results.

Each data set played an important role. And while it seems obvious these three sets would be linked in order to offer valuable, accurate insights ... *none were*! These teams never met to discuss or review projections. With zero integration, the organization boasted a wealth of data but little meaningful or actionable information. Among ridiculous ways to misuse data, this stood apart. Might we wonder why the company found itself in a cash crunch and sitting on too much inventory?

Unfortunately, I could share many more horror stories of companies making poor (or no) use of sales data. Consider the owner at one distributor client who bought an iPad for each member of the sales team. Why? To access a CRM? To allow the team to access data remotely? No. He had used one in a choir group and thought they were *cool*. Without offering resources, tools, and functionality to contribute to salespeople's productivity—and without exploring how such tools might facilitate access to critical data—this huge purchase proved nothing more than a giant waste of money.

Unless you think critically about business data—how you collect it and use it to drive decision-making—you're destined to make similar mistakes that run the gamut between wasteful and disastrous. **You *must* follow a deliberate, carefully considered effort to translate data into information and insight.** Otherwise, you hold little more than a bunch of numbers likely to yield only inaccuracies, faulty conclusions, and underwhelming results.

I witness too many companies mismanaging both internal and external data. Some use faulty metrics in-house and thus fail to grow their business. Others communicate data incorrectly to buyers, which generates customer service problems and costs the company sales.

Let's take a closer look at these mistakes, beginning with the issue plaguing the apparel company in our opening anecdote: siloed data.

Siloed Data Is Poison

Keeping your data siloed, as did the three teams who forgot to share—proves downright poisonous. Many companies today still fail to embrace a data-centric approach to sales. According to LinkedIn's 2020 "State of Sales," 50 percent of sellers and companies still use no data to assess sellers or evaluate patterns in business won or lost.[20] Worse, not integrating data among sales, marketing, and customer service typically leads to false results; in short, you perceive your team as more successful than it is. You fail to recognize your reality: too many, too poor, or too few leads; inaccurate retention rates; product profitability not in line with actual results; or trends that need to be corrected or leveraged. Each such outcome proves destructive, if not catastrophic.

For example, a marketing team must understand both the quality of each lead and the quantity needed to accomplish sales goals. If the team uncovers a massive volume of leads that salespeople can't access, failure becomes pretty much a sure thing.

That's precisely what happened to a client in financial services. The organization developed a solid marketing process to sell to banks that would help them develop highly targeted leads

---

20   "The LinkedIn State of Sales Report 2020," January 2021, https://business. linkedin.com/content/dam/me/business/en-us/sales-solutions/resources/pdfs/ state-of-sales_pocketguide_r11_v2.pdf.

of new prospects seeking loans and mortgages. My client excited customers and won deals by promising to double the leads coming in. What's more, they delivered in spades—customers found themselves buried in piles of new leads. And therein lay the problem: the bank's loan officers became so overwhelmed by the onslaught, they could only close half of these hot prospects. With too few staff to deliver, conversations slowed and new sales stagnated. The projects failed. The lesson here is this: if you build a strategy based solely on sales data and neglect to consider data associated with your organizational capabilities, success may well elude you.

Poor-quality leads prove catastrophic for businesses. For example, marketing programs that target gatekeepers rather than decision makers bloat workloads for sellers while yielding disastrously low ROI. At the same time, programs centered on the wrong people also see underwhelming results. A medical software company made a particularly painful error. Their marketing materials boasted how their software could pare down both IT costs and nursing headcounts. Based on fresh data, they took their pitch to IT and nursing departments—the very people they were promising to replace. Had the company made their case to the CFO—who had an incentive to consider the software's ability to reduce salary costs—they may have found a more receptive audience.

Having too *few* leads is also a problem. For example, a marketing department with whom I've worked provided only enough funding in their annual budget to cover *half* the leads the sales team needed to hit targets. This was based on an invalid assumption about closing costs.

In each of these examples, companies failed on two levels: they lacked the right data, and then they siloed the inadequate research. Had they compared and compiled what each had, they would quickly understand which numbers didn't add up and could avoid lost sales and wasted time.

Integrate Data to Improve Sales and Retention

"Gone are the days of relying only on intuition to guide decisions," announces the LinkedIn 2020 "State of Sales" report. To ensure success, you must now access timely and relevant data. This same report shares an insight from Joseph DiMisa, a sales effectiveness and rewards leader at Korn Ferry: "Sales organizations with a clear data strategy for their go-to-market efforts reported that 11% more of their sellers made goal and they won forecasted deals 8% more of the time."[21]

You must share data and information across departments to generate insights. When you do it right—with data points integrated throughout your organization—you no longer risk becoming a victim of bad data. Instead, you gain tools needed to improve sales and retention.

Let's jump in and look at ways to get a handle on your data, to share it wisely, and to use it to your advantage.

Using Negative Data Positively: Create an Early Warning System

Collect the right data and draw the appropriate conclusions from it. Do this and you create an early warning system to alert

---

21 Ibid.

you to any risk that buyers may leave you for a competitor. Most companies use "big data" to locate and target offers to new buyers—but the smartest also use "little data"—targeted, specific indicators—to understand customer behavior and to forecast inaccuracy, buyer disengagement, market stagnation, and profit-margin erosion. **You cannot grow your business unless you can first predict losses.**

Being Right on the Money means holding onto existing customers while gaining market share. If you can home in on early indicators a buyer may be contemplating a switch, you can move to prevent this loss while still pursuing growth.

This is why I created the Engage Early Warning System for clients in the business software sector, where buyers are notoriously fickle. This powerful tool predicts 85 percent of cases where a client stands to lose a customer. You can build your own early warning system and hold on to more business as you grow. Here's how:

First review all customers lost over the last two years and look at your behavior patterns with each. My system identifies more than two dozen specific traits and then pinpoints those by posing three categories of questions:

- **What were buyers doing?** Buyers' actions tell us plenty if we pay careful attention. If even one buyer left you, determine why. Also look at what happened before their departure. Had buying already slowed or stopped?
- **How engaged were they?** You cannot influence anyone who opts not to listen. Open your CRM. What key activities, contacts, and marketing opportunities did you

harness? Examine the quality and quantity of communication between you and your former buyer. Had they stopped returning calls? Had interactions with your customer support team slowed or ceased entirely?

- **What does your data say?** Numbers yield facts and create deeper understanding. Look at the buyer's most recent purchasing history. Was the annual value of transactions with the buyer increasing or decreasing?

When you have the answers to those questions, crunch the numbers. The next stage in the Engage Selling Early Warning System is analytical. We use mathematical tools to determine which factors signal account risk and how much weight to apply to each. Our analytical tool predicts customer losses with great success because it considers specific behavioral traits:

- decreasing annual buyer value;
- decreasing deployment of new sites;
- fewer customer support cases opened;
- fewer sales-related activities reported in the CRM, such as inbound/outbound calls and appointments; and
- fewer new contacts created in the CRM for a particular buyer.

Once we identify and assign a relative weight to these factors, we calculate a score for each account, thus defining the threshold of risk for buyer defection. Equipped with such data, you can take action to protect those buyers most at risk of leaving.

Use Data Wisely for Growth Insights

Collecting and studying data prevents losses and can help you pinpoint new growth opportunities, but only if you approach the task with wisdom. Alas, many don't. Some boast how they track everything but cannot point to any inherent logic—they lack any clear idea of what may be important and meaningful. Without a plan, the data does little to help you make the right decisions.

Let's look at this issue in action. The first scenario is common: buyers get into the habit of collecting "vanity" metrics, that is, they track items that lack any value.

Vanity Metrics

In my field work, I encounter countless sales VPs blindly in love with vanity metrics—meaningless variables that offer no real information to help align practices with strategy.

Typically, they lead with, "We track everything. We've got more data than we know what to do with."

"Great," I respond. "Show me what you're looking at."

Next, I find myself staring at spreadsheet after spreadsheet of numbers—but with no insights about whether or not the team is successful. For instance, a VP of sales may track the number of calls each day and applaud those doing the most dialing— even if each call lasts only thirty seconds and does nothing to drive sales. Meanwhile, the person who makes five calls, spends four hours on the phone, and lands three new deals receives little to no credit, since vanity metrics overlook their success.

One coaching client—let's call him Dave—called me, quite upset. After bringing in $10 million in sales—well past his $7 million quota—he found himself reprimanded by his boss. How did this happen?

In Dave's business, sellers typically spend much of their time logging miles from one in-person client meeting to another. His was classified as an essential service even during the COVID lockdowns. The VP of sales identified and tracked mileage as the most valuable metric of productivity and success. Dave racked up the lowest number of miles on his team. Why? Instead of spending hours in his car, he devised new strategies that required much less time behind the wheel: using email, connecting with buyers via social media, bringing them to him, dropping things in the mail—all to great success! He deepened relationships with many buyers while being more efficient, thanks in part to technology. Dave brought in the most revenue that year—even setting a record—but because his boss focused solely on distance logged as a measure of success, he received a firm talking-to when what he deserved was a big congratulations. **Mileage represents a prime example of a vanity metric—it offers no information about what a seller does to achieve great results.** Companies frequently look to the number of proposals made as another measure of effectiveness, but this, too, poses a problem. Quantity reveals nothing about the *value* of those proposals or whether they help boost sales. We need to consider what those numbers really mean and what they tell us about quality. If the answer is nothing, know you have a vanity metric on your hands that's probably doing little for you. Let's look at some of the most common vanity metrics.

- **Social media metrics:** These are a hot topic. Many companies track Facebook fans, Twitter followers, blog-post page views, email-opening rates, and LinkedIn connections—measures of the *quantity* of engagement with customers and other audiences. A broad social media presence does, of course, matter, but the *quality* of engagement tells you much more. Followers, fans, views, and likes prove meaningful only if they inspire your target audience to interact with you, send messages, make comments, ask questions, or share additional content. Such active interactions convert to leads.

- **Seller vanity metrics:** These phony productivity metrics—call attempts, reaches, connect duration, and opportunity creation—serve only to pump up egos. **Quantitative metrics trump qualitative measures when it comes to your buyer.** For example, measuring the number of call attempts tells you nothing unless you know how many times you must dial to hit your goal. To transform vanity metrics into more valuable insights, start by understanding the activities sellers undertake to hit goals based on their average annual closing rate, then work backward to determine the number of calls, connects, and opportunities that stand behind that success.

- **Benchmark vanity metrics:** Companies typically compare their sellers to the average—but *average* should never be your goal. Instead compare each member of your sales team to the very best player. What does each need to do to replicate the top performer's results? Considering this question moves benchmarking beyond mirror-gazing to something meaningful.

Understand What You Need to Measure and Why

While faulty or meaningless data presents real hurdles, so, too, does an unclear strategy around what to measure. I recently took a call from a business owner who asked me to train his sales team, which he described simply as "terrible."

I laughed. "What evidence do you have?"

"Simple—we *never* hit our targets," he grumbled.

Before I agreed to help, I scanned the data he shared. The sales team was actually closing 70 percent of leads—contrary to his belief, they were *great* closers. Their real problem turned out to be lead generation. Even with a stellar close rate, they attracted only enough leads to hit 75 percent of their target.

Instead of harvesting insights from the data, this leader had followed his gut—and equated falling short of targets with failures in closing. The fix proved simple: by concentrating on doubling leads, they could also double sales.

Follow the Buyer's Lead

Sales data becomes much more meaningful and actionable when it captures the voice of your buyers. Raw sales data may paint your sales team as a runaway success, and yet behind the scenes, customers may shape quite a different picture. For example, one aerospace client lauded themselves for turning around quotes within forty-eight hours—only to find out buyers expected to hear back in half this time. A deeper dive revealed many such benchmarks missed the mark, which in turn meant lost orders.

When my client asked customers what they considered important and then refocused policies and practices on meeting those expectations, sales increased and customers stuck around.

After you separate the data wheat from the chaff and target what is important and why, what's next? The answer may surprise you. You need to micromanage. Seriously.

Micromanaging Isn't Bad—It's Required

The most revered tropes on leadership all preach some variation of a common theme: never micromanage, because doing so limits productivity and often proves downright annoying. Here I dare to defy the accepted wisdom: **throw out any notions micromanaging is bad—in fact, when working with data, micromanaging is a must.**

To clarify, when I encourage micromanaging, in no way am I proposing you start nagging your people over meaningless minutiae (see "annoying," above). Instead, I urge you to hold sales team members accountable for how they choose, collect, and use data, and of course for their results.

Consider an example that demonstrates the power—and necessity—of burrowing into the nitty-gritty of data. I worked with two start-up companies with a solid foothold in their markets and who stood poised to take off. But sales at both had fallen, and each VP felt caught in the crosshairs. The owners and boards of directors studied the numbers and asked questions for which these VPs lacked answers. They failed to realize the pipeline was so far off track they stood no chance to hit targets. Worse, when asked how they could get back on a winning path, both offered the same flaccid excuse. "I'm a hands-off kind of guy. Our salespeople know what they're doing, so I let them figure it out and follow up from time to time."

Clearly, though, the VPs were staying *too* hands-off. Unfamiliar with the numbers, the territories, and the deals, they lacked any benchmarks to help their teams do better. When in a position of responsibility, choosing to stay hands-off also means absolving yourself from holding your team accountable. In essence, you force your sales team to manage itself. As you might expect, these VPs soon moved from "hands off" to "laid off."

Micromanaging concentrates on handling the smallest details and on asking the toughest questions, the kind no one else bothers with or that your team hopes you won't ask because the answers might create more work.

Think of the top players in professional sports—Steph Curry, LeBron James, and Tom Brady, for example. They may seem like lone wolves, but take a closer look: by contrast, they're overcoached and micromanaged to the max. The granularity of attention they receive allows both them and the team to soar. The same goes for a sales team. When you become intimate with all aspects of your best player's portfolio, you can not only help that player win big, but you can propagate that "A-team" talent and skills to other members of your sales team. The whole crew stays Right on the Money.

Even after considering the arguments I offer, some may still bristle at the notion of micromanaging. It may seem at odds with how you like to work. I would argue that if you shy away from asking the hard questions, and if you feel you can best hold your team to the highest standard by keeping your distance, you throw your own career and future into an uncertain light. After all, how will you defend your track record, your approach and, ultimately, your results when your CEO puts *you* to the test?

Ask probing, purposeful questions. Because such productive micromanaging reveals the straightest track to your team's performance issues and yet-to-be-tapped potential.

Match up these insights with your data. What gaps do we face? What strengths and weaknesses must we bolster or overcome? What qualities captured and secured our biggest deals—and which seem most at risk? What business looks likely to close? What's our upside and downside? Unless you continue to capture direct and satisfying answers to these and other questions, you do little more than take shots in the dark.

All the best sales managers have become masterful micromanagers. This is no coincidence. **Sales management is a science, and like all science, it operates on hard questions and real data rather than wishes and assumptions.**

Getting Right on the Money: Quick Tip

As you dive into your data—both little and big—strive to balance the qualitative and the quantitative, because both prove important. Tell me you make twenty-five calls to land a sale, and I'll tell you I don't care. I want to know *who* you're calling and what information you seek. What products are you targeting? What problems do you hope to uncover, and how can you solve them? Too often, sales VPs assume the person *doing* the most—attending the most meetings, drafting the most proposals, and firing off the most emails—must also be the top producer. Alas, because *quality* of activity matters at least as much as volume, you may discover being the busiest may not mean being the best (just ask poor Dave).

When you study patterns and norms in how your team works, look also for anomalies. For example, who on the team is producing better results with less work? Hint: the data that really matters comes from your top two performers. As we discussed previously, when you hold the entire team to the standard set by top performers rather than strive for "average," you move the needle for all.

Don't Forget about Finance

While you muscle through your sales data "spring cleaning," you may also find your company's finances to be overdue for a data-driven reality check. Too many companies focus on revenue. Look also at profits—and more specifically, train the spotlight on your most profitable products. A small-business client of mine shared her shock upon discovering her company had lost money for the very first time. At first glance the data suggested all was well—with 60 percent of revenue coming from one popular product. Unfortunately, a quick look at her revenue data revealed the production and sales process was eating through all of that lucrative revenue. To keep your revenue and other finances Right on the Money, merge financial data with information coming from your sales team.

Convert Insights to Instant Sales

Another client discovered 90 percent of sales came from just 30 percent of products. By culling just half of the bottom-performing products (they remain scared to go all the way), they reduced inventory, increased cash flow, and showcased a more cohesive collection to clients—one that sells out quickly.

This client generates new top buyers just by looking for—and learning from—how existing top buyers behave and then using this information to influence the "next-best ten." Everyone wants to be the best, so when you tap into this desire—with real data to back you up—customers follow suit.

Employ this same technique to drive your own sales. First look at what your best customers buy and how they buy it. From there examine their decision-making path. Which product or product category did they first buy? Who made the purchase? How did their buying grow from that point forward?

Then identify the *next-best* set of customers—those approaching the buying behaviors of your top tier. Replicate your successful actions with existing buyers to move these "tier twos" to the top. Don't be shy to share data. Tell this second tier how your best buyers do X, Y, or Z. Let them know how those buyers benefit from your products and services. Use this technique for upselling, cross-selling, and retention.

Here is another best practice: share with buyers information about how others are thinking ahead. For example, one client constantly shares with his customer base that the company's best buyers purchase six months in advance. Follow his lead and watch sales blossom.

Employ Predictive Analytics to Ensure Forecast Accuracy

Predictive analytics help your sales team capture the most accurate forecasts. We start with the familiar sales pipeline that transforms opportunities into wins or losses through stages, including discovery, qualification, solution design, customer evaluation, proposal delivery, and negotiation. Your goal is to make each stage improve chances of securing sales.

We need this elementary-level sales refresher because many confuse *pipelines* with *forecasts*, or they recognize no real difference between the two—a big problem. **To attain true sales predictability, you must study pipelines and forecasts independently and ensure your pipeline numbers influence your forecast output.**

A sales pipeline captures a snapshot of all *opportunities* and must illustrate everything from newly identified prospects to those ready to close. A forecast, on the other hand, centers on a smaller segment of your pipeline and predicts expected revenue through a specific time period. Many sellers fail when they concentrate only on middle and later stages of pipelines (e.g., proposal delivery and negotiation) and ignore the top end of unqualified leads.

This shortcoming happens because sellers often use subjective measurements rather than objective measures when they evaluate their pipelines. Leaders often gauge the relative strength of sales pipelines by the probability of deals closing. This is a mistake. Probability of close is a subjective measurement that requires sellers to advance judgments about chances of making a sale. Since such guesswork is rife with misinterpretation and bias, it's also rich in potential for abuse. Every week I hear stories about sellers who refuse to act on opportunities in their CRM because they can't be certain a sale is going to close. Rather than risk being held accountable for all leads, they think it better for them (and less likely to encourage coaching) if they put only "real" leads in the system. They want close ratios to appear robust and falsely think all opportunities must become part of their forecast. Thus, they avoid documenting uncertain opportunities. Such behavior makes gauging pipeline health impossible and prevents you from doing the following:

- accurately predicting future revenue;
- understanding lead conversion ratios;
- objectively coaching your team and analyzing strengths and weaknesses; and
- implementing strategies to improve your team and your pipeline.

Stacking opportunities at the top of the pipeline means little or nothing about those opportunities being certain to close; instead, it reveals the true quantity of opportunities in the marketplace and helps you measure conversion ratios at every stage. Ultimately, this discipline enables you to create forecasts that accurately reflect your revenue potential from well-qualified opportunities.

If you accept the importance of capturing all opportunities in the top end of your pipeline, even if you lack a crystal ball into whether or not they will eventually close, you can then adopt a nuance sure to strengthen your pipeline management process: **stop talking about *probability of close* at each stage of the pipeline and start talking about *percentage complete* in the sales cycle.**

As you progress through your pipeline, every stage represents both a step completed and a step just beginning. As a sales leader, you want to see your team moving deals through the pipeline, completing each stage properly, and gradually progressing toward wins.

When opportunities advance to a next stage, the percentage complete increases. And when opportunities evolve to the point you consider them "fully qualified,", experience shows you may safely assume one-third will close. This calculation will yield your forecast based on data and not your seller bias.

This change demands a shift in thinking. Saying a negotiation is 90-percent complete no longer means the opportunity is 90-percent certain to close. It simply means you've completed nearly all activities required to seal the deal. Keep in mind that you may only close 30 or 40 percent of the deals that are in this stage—something you can anticipate based on past data. But whatever your actual close rate is at this stage, it will be objectively based and provable, not based on a subjective feeling someone has about the quality of the opportunity.

Every step of the sales process consists of tasks or activities you must complete to propel the deal through the pipeline, to solidify from subjective to objective. If the team properly employs the pipeline, managers gain a truly accurate read on conversion ratios between one stage and the next. From there you can create an accurate forecast.

By arriving at your forecast number through an objective measurement—percentage complete—rather than the far more subjective "probability to close," your forecasts become much more accurate, and you gain an objective coaching tool to use in meetings and reviews. Best of all, this pipeline model spares you the highs and lows afflicting most sales organizations—what I call "sales whiplash."

The bottom line is this: **Create revenue transparency, consistency, and predictability by controlling your data. This mission-critical task will save your sanity.**

Data Tricks Learned along the Way

One crucial lesson from my decades in sales is that it takes twice as long to lose a sale as it does to win one. In other words, if it takes you ninety days to move a piece of business from the top of your pipeline through to close, you will know at roughly 180 days you've lost your chance of securing that business. Somewhere between ninety and 180 days, you can spot real evidence in your data that things are going awry. When you learn to find these indicators, you free up a tremendous amount of time, and your team can move on to more promising leads.

Most sellers usually hang on to things for too long—mostly because they're competitive and they lack sufficient leads. But if you can use your data to demonstrate that their tendency to cling to long shots isn't doing them any favors, they can refocus that time on tasks that offer more potential.

To determine when to move on, look at the number of times you move the close date. Once the customer begins to say, "Call me back next month," or, "Reach out next quarter," you're heading toward a loss. Once you've heard such pushback five times, the deal is dead. With this in mind, you can figure out roughly when the buyer is saying no; you can then coach your team on how to avoid such losses while teaching them to recognize the time to move on.

Sellers and leaders make common mistakes in how they collect and employ business data, including keeping information siloed, tracking the wrong items, and trusting one's misguided gut feelings over cold, hard facts. Once you understand why data is so important—and what it can help you accomplish— you gain the upper hand and can radically improve performance. Your next step is to help your team employ such tactics to pump up their results. To do this, you must become more than a sales manager—you must become a coach.

Chapter 9

BUILD AND GROW
A COACHING CULTURE

Success in sales today hinges on building and sustaining a coaching culture within your organization. From my experience those who coach their people three or more hours each month can count on a performance boost of up to 30 percent.

Effective coaching extends beyond in-class instruction. A recent Gartner study offers two jarring insights into where salespeople learn today. Up to 66 percent of salespeople say they pick up most of what they learn outside the classroom, and 70 percent of sales leaders feel low confidence in their ability to translate strategy into action.[22] When you coach you help sellers take concepts learned in class or from books and apply them in the real world under the guidance of a person committed to holding them accountable and showing them how to improve constantly.

---

22   "How Sales Leaders Lead through Disruption," Gartner, January 2021, https://www.gartner.com/en/sales/insights/sales-leaders-lead-through-disruption.

As sales manager your role is to teach and refine each seller's skills, so they become the best at what they do—and stay there. You accomplish this not by managing them (job title or no)—you get there by coaching them.

Coaching someone to become a top seller is tricky. Your biggest impediment is, well ... you. Your ascent to management likely rewarded your reputation as a top seller rather than any promise you demonstrated in managing and coaching, which require completely different skill sets. Being great at one in no way means excelling in the other. As a newly promoted sales VP, I thought it absurd for a sales manager to step into that role without solid frontline experience; over time, though, I've learned many of the best sales leaders spend very little time in the sales trenches. Why? Great coaches know they're exactly where they're meant to be.

Think about hockey (I'm Canadian, after all). Wayne Gretzky created utter magic on the ice and proved a complete flop as a coach. On the flip side, many of the NHL's most gifted coaches were—at best—average hockey players. The same is true for sales—some prove to be a "natural" at closing deals, while others excel at guiding the success of others.

Here is another challenge: nearly every seller-turned-manager I encounter, upon moving up in position, struggles to let go of previous responsibilities that led to their success—their "glory days." Adding people responsibilities to their job description does nothing to quell the desire and drive to sell. Tacking on responsibility for leading others creates the most highly dysfunctional seller-manager dynamic possible.

Know this: once you enter management, you must turn over all accounts and throw all your energy into coaching. Your team must be greater than any individual and must acquire and strengthen any skills that are lacking. According to the Objective Management Group and their study of over three million sellers and sales managers, the best sales managers spend fully 70 percent of their time—more than two of every three hours—coaching, motivating, and training.

Too many sales managers continue to retain their company's biggest, most strategic accounts. Since they make money selling to those accounts, other sellers assume these managers are padding their nests by hoarding the best deals. What's more, the sales team sees the manager putting sales ahead of managing and coaching, **a near-impossible task for one attempting to both manage people and service accounts**. The team feels neglected, and important things begin to fall away.

Top performers take this the hardest. Who wants to work with someone competing with you? This awkward circumstance makes it hard to believe your leader holds your best interests at heart—a conundrum guaranteed to foment animosity.

I allow for one exception to my rule of managers not owning their own clients: in a start-up environment with a new team and less than two years of revenue, there may be no choice but to have players serve as coaches too. Even then, though, you must work toward building a team where leaders lead, and players play. Alas, once companies move past start-up mode, owners and executives often believe they cannot afford for the sales manager to stop selling, or they feel the relationships a new manager worked hard to cultivate are worth them spending their energy on, rather than on coaching sellers.

One client in the consumer products industry struggles with this very problem. The sales manager holds responsibility for managing salespeople but also clings to premium and strategic accounts. The business owner has been pushing the manager for more than a year to pass the accounts along but keeps hearing these excuses:

- The team will be distracted if I give them these accounts.
- The accounts are low-margin and high maintenance.
- The clients know me best and don't want to deal with anyone else.
- It's easier for me to manage them than teach someone else the ins and outs.

To some, such arguments may sound convincing; to me all this reveals is an opportunity to train a team to take on this work. The manager can pass the accounts over; he just chooses not to. To make matters worse, the team is about one million dollars short of sales targets—a nightmare of which the manager was unaware until recently because his full attention focused on accounts he could never relinquish.

This manager is no isolated example. In fact, when I transitioned from selling into a sales VP role at Open Text, I also refused to give up marquee accounts, and I offered many of the same excuses. I was lucky to work for a very smart leader who simply cut off access to my accounts in the CRM and assigned them to someone else. The message was clear: my boss needed me to be a full-time sales leader, not a part-time seller.

Recognize it is up to you to make every seller on your team better than you were and to learn how to use those top sellers to the team's advantage. Replace your glory days as a leader in sales with new ones as a leader of people. In sales leadership today, that's the only way to be Right on the Money.

Expect Results

Far too many leaders fall short at another crucial coaching skill: communicating expectations. As I routinely point out, no other job would allow half of its workforce to perform below expectations, and yet here we are: only 54 percent of salespeople hit their targets each year. If your manufacturing teams churned out only half of needed product, you would soon cut them loose; if your drivers only delivered half of their orders, same story. But we have long given sellers a pass. No more!

In this new performance-management culture, we no longer accept subpar outcomes. We expect all sellers to achieve 100 percent of results. While it may seem impossible for all to hit targets, I assure you: they can. I've seen it happen again and again.

One client recently saw each of its sellers hit goals by establishing targets very thoughtfully based on the previous year's results, market expectations, growth projections, and competitor research. The company's board of directors set the targets based on input from investors, company leaders, and the sales team's own assessment of market conditions. By being so thorough, the board ensured the VP of sales could in no way "game the system" to create desired results; the outcomes were *real*. This is no anomaly: another client recently achieved 100-percent results with everyone who'd been with the company for a year or longer. These examples demonstrate that **when your expectations are Right on the Money, so, too, will be your results.**

Investigate Your Lineup

Setting realistic yet ambitious expectations propels you in the right direction, but this can take you only so far. If your team fails to meet such standards, you must find out why. Sometimes the players themselves are the issue—if so, move them out. Sales managers too often rationalize that partially productive sellers are better than none at all. Nonsense! Each seller consistently missing the mark creates opportunities for the competition to move in on those buyers. The more excuses a manager allows, the lazier sellers become and the more business heads to your competitors. And once you lose a customer, good luck winning them back.

The real reason managers cling to this deadwood is that they fail to recruit and coach consistently or efficiently. Hold everyone—managers as well as sellers—accountable for results, and make it clear none will stick around should they fail to perform.

I developed the tool below to support clients as massive as Chevron and Experian and as small as pet supply company RC Pets. It provides a framework to reflect on relative strengths and shortcomings in your recruitment and development of salespeople. For example, it encourages you to assess whether your players genuinely lack potential, or you should instead take a closer look at your coaching skills.

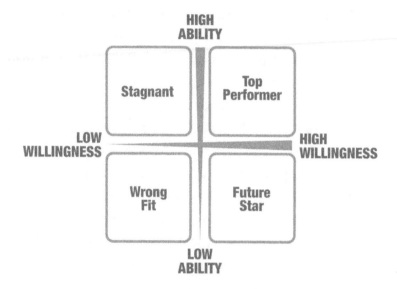

As the tool shows, willingness reflects attitude or self-motivation; ability means skill. Do your sellers know what to say on a call? Do they understand your value proposition? Can they discuss the finer points of each product or service? While we can build skills through a host of interventions such as training and coaching, we can only assess and develop *willingness* through a personalized approach. This requires follow-up and personal accountability and is best served by one-on-one coaching and mentoring. To assess willingness, you must be able to ask frankly: *Does the seller **want** to do what's required to be successful?*

The best coaching always builds on assessments of both willingness and ability. Where you position your sellers on the chart determines whether you can boost their results with a coaching strategy or it's time to say goodbye. Let's take a closer look at where sellers tend to fall and reflect on what this means for your coaching plan:

- **High willingness and high ability:** Salespeople demonstrating both traits are your superstars. They know exactly what needs to be done and how to do it, *and* they put in the work to make it happen. They constantly address both their attitude and their skill set. While it's a mistake to leave them alone (more on this in a moment), for players like these, a refined coaching approach aimed at capturing best practices should be your focus.

- **High willingness and low ability:** These young upstarts are always pleading, "Put me in, coach!" Willing to try new things, they as yet lack the refined skills to do all that needs to be done. They may just need to learn all your products or to internalize your value proposition, both of which you can address with training. Here coaching works its magic—happy to try anything, this group takes on tasks that lead to real growth. Consider Grace, a young seller with whom I work. While I regularly provide workshops for forty of her colleagues, only Grace reaches out after every session to ask questions and gain new insights. She actively participates on every webinar, even sending real-life scenarios for which she seeks my opinion on her chosen approach. It's no surprise Grace is ramping up in her territory and finds herself on track to exceed targets faster than any other new team member.

- **Low willingness and high ability:** I worry about these stagnant sellers the most because they present the biggest coaching conundrum. Seasoned vets with twenty to thirty years of experience often find themselves in this situation—long successful at doing things a certain way, they watch such success wane because they refuse to embrace new approaches. As they see fewer results, they double down and do *more* of what was already failing. If one hundred cold calls fall flat, two hundred should be the charm. Soon they grow tired and cranky before completely burning out. Your challenge? Remotivate them and help get their valuable historical knowledge working for them again—but only if they commit to the work necessary to make it in sales today.

• **Low willingness and low ability:** Some on your team may simply end up being the wrong fit—unwilling or unable to take steps that lead to success. You cannot just bench them—you must kick them off the team. While you can recognize ability with ease, gauging willingness may prove more daunting. At the end of a coaching call or meeting, after you agree on next steps, see how players act. Do they attempt to tackle their list? Do they persist if they try and fail? Willingness to learn *must* be present, because those with the wrong attitude will always offer an excuse rather than see things through. When you see a pattern—a list of why they failed to deliver—show them the door.

Coach like a Champ

I routinely offer strategies to help boost the skills of those new to coaching or who have yet to see the results they pursue. All involve three core elements: **pipeline building, opportunity management, and skill strengthening**. As we explored through our discussion of Sales Velocity in chapter 6, sellers must constantly evaluate whether their pipeline is big enough for them to hit goals. They also need to assess the likelihood of closing opportunities and to pinpoint areas where they remain stuck. And they must discern whether or not they carry the requisite skills to implement their sales process. As coach you must help sellers consistently weigh each factor.

Unfortunately, despite the effectiveness of targeted coaching, many companies push sellers into workshops and other training sessions that may well be the least effective—and for some, the *worst*—place to acquire needed skills. I'll explain.

From my experience, when sellers struggle to apply new concepts and practices, they lack context. Scenarios presented at workshops feel too abstract or too distant. By contrast, the problem currently knocking at their door makes them sit up and pay attention.

The faster learners can apply a new tactic, the more readily it becomes part of them and their work. To facilitate this, **you must foster an accelerated learning environment**.

Instead of barraging your team with more workshops and more ideas from the outside, harness insights around what works well from top performers *inside* your organization and leverage those strategies for greater success.

Also give thought to your timing. Since you no longer focus on your own accounts, you can orchestrate an ideal coaching environment for each team member. The content of your conversations, while important, carries little more weight than the amount of time you put in.

You're in luck—I know the magic number: three hours monthly per rep, in the form of one-on-one sessions every other week. Each session must last thirty minutes to an hour and focus on discussing strengths and weaknesses regarding the pipeline, opportunities, or skills—whatever the individual needs most. Spend time each month listening in on calls or joining sellers on ride-alongs. Add hourly group meetings each week and consider other formal opportunities for sellers to learn from each other.

Let's take a closer look at these strategies in action.

One-on-One Coaching

One-on-one coaching enables managers to hold private conversations with sales reps and to analyze and discuss issues you would prefer not to share with the rest of the team. You must stay objective; otherwise, the seller thinks managers provide feedback only when they catch sellers doing something wrong. Instead of taking feedback to heart, a cornered seller tends to check out or ignore any input. To ensure coaching feels objective, do the following:

1. Set a consistent schedule, such as Mondays at 9:00 a.m. With a standing check-in time, sellers know what to expect rather than feel they're being hauled into your office for a talking-to. Setting schedules pulls out the emotions and drives engagement.

2. Start your coaching sessions with a quick recap of the following:
    -   the seller's results to date;
    -   results the seller must achieve to get back on track; and
    -   the difference between the two (positive or negative).

3. Ask questions. Specifically:
   - How will you make up the difference?
   - What should we do to leverage success?
   - What have you tried and how did it work?
   - What are you not doing today that you need to do more of in the next month?
   - What's working well for you right now?
4. Offer advice, with choices and examples:
   - I think you should try this … What do you think?
   - Strategy X works well for Mary in the northeast territory. Would that work for you?
   - In the past you enjoyed great success with ABC. Should we go back to doing that?
5. Wrap up with action steps. Coaching concentrates on creating behavioral change. If you finish the session without focusing on what the seller will do differently as a result of your conversation, nothing will change. The key is to ensure sellers buy in to action steps by having *them*—not you—communicate what will be done.
   - Based on what we discussed, what will you do differently this week?
   - Of all ideas shared, what will you implement?
   - How will you put this into practice?

As managers wrap up one-to-one coaching sessions, they should remember to never let a seller choose more than three items to implement. Doing so leads to overwhelm and implementation fail. Also, you must always set a follow-up plan to hold sellers accountable for implementing what they promise.

After all, if a sales manager fails to follow up to ensure the work gets done, who will?

Ride-Along Coaching

We promote ride-along coaching not to save sales, nor to turn the manager into a closing hero. We don't do it to fix mistakes during a sale. This would work only to make you a helicopter manager, sure to demoralize your staff. In fact, ride-along coaching helps you listen and observe now so that you might help your seller learn and apply lessons later.

To "ride along" and collect evidence on how each seller performs with each buyer, you can listen in on a live call (held by phone or video conference—so no "ride" at all) or hop into a car beside a seller and head to a meeting—observing all required social distancing rules, of course. Perhaps you do this already. Managers tell me they ride along with sellers all the time, but when I join in, I often watch a manager not just heading out to quietly observe and later provide feedback. Instead, they behave as though they'd just donned a superhero cape— all ready to swoop in and "save the day." To them, a manager's real goal is to serve as Super Seller, shouting: "Let me show you how it's done!" They then imagine themselves wowing the crowd with their superhero selling powers. In reality, though … none of this is helpful.

Tough as it may be, tuck your cape away. On a ride-along, your sole job is to observe the seller in action and gather evidence for a useful debrief on what works and what doesn't. You must do this—and only this—because you can't coach without evidence.

Learning by Doing

Learning by doing tops the list of the most effective skills coaching can bolster—a bold statement, sure, but working on skills with your manager in a live setting ensures near-universal success. Simply put, "learning by doing" starts when coaches or sellers identify areas that need development and assign related activities.

For instance, if a team member needs to work on presentation skills, you ask them to pick an opportunity ready for a presentation. To prepare, assign various readings, identify activities to practice, and note where planning is needed. Next provide one-on-one coaching by inviting the seller into your office for an hour to review ways they prepared, to conduct a roleplay of the interaction, and to refine their approach.

In this example, consider role-playing both the presentation and any questions or objections the seller may face. When the seller returns from the client, have them prepare a debrief of what worked and what they would tackle differently. Finally, carve out next steps with the seller for ongoing implementation and improvement.

Team Sales Meetings

Team sales meetings play an important role in updating the team on products and services while offering a platform for brainstorming solutions to any challenges or conundrums sellers may bring. For instance, a seller might share a need for help navigating a stuck deal. With many minds on a video call, or in person, your team can uncover other opportunities and avenues a single seller may well miss.

In addition, people can share individual successes so the rest of the team can learn. When they discuss what works for them—for example, how they closed a piece of business, along with other factors that led to success—the rest of the team will feel inspired to adopt similar winning strategies.

Sellers at one client struggled with a skill the manager considered basic: how to build rapport and personalize. She fell short each time she endeavored to convey such simple concepts to her team.

"Look," I told her, "Bring this up in a sales meeting. Get all those brains on it. To defuse any pressure, tell them each is just throwing out ideas, with no such thing as a bad one. And forbid responding with, 'Yes, but …' or 'That'll never work.' Instead, the team must build on items thrown into the conversation."

Although hesitant she agreed to try and soon became a true believer once the team generated dozens of solid, implementable ideas. As we learned in a previous chapter, creativity flourishes in a group setting. Plus, sellers respond best to peers, another strength you can harness through formalized peer coaching.

Formalized Peer Coaching

Asking your best to teach the rest sits at the heart of being Right on the Money. Ambitious sellers seek mentors, and a formalized peer-coaching program offers powerful, experienced, and trusted support. Be careful, though! Don't yank your top performers out of the field—this will just drive them crazy and sling your organization into dysfunction. The same goes for pairing top performers with those flailing at the bottom. No one wants to babysit a poor performer! However, consider these tried-and-true strategies to turn peer coaching into a performance generator.

- **Have top performers present during sales meetings.** Make full use of their presence at those meetings you already require them to attend. This offers an ideal time for sales leaders to share what's working and what's winning, to inspire peers from top to bottom without stressing anyone out.

- **Partner top performers with number twos.** When you pair top performers with other successful sellers, they seldom feel you're wasting their time or messing with their schedule; instead they typically become ready and eager to share ideas. A day of shadowing—where the top performer pursues a regular day and invites an observer along—proves highly effective. Many times a shadow with major potential soon shares the number-one spot. An important note: know the differences between top performers before you partner them—this must be deliberate, not piecemeal, and offer the chance to coach your top players into peers and continue the chain of helping sellers meet their ultimate potential.

- **Onboarding.** The faster someone completes training and is ready to go, the sooner they can contribute to your success. To drive this point home, one client once challenged his team, "I want us to *halve* the time it takes for someone to be productive." His existing onboarding process cost him $300,000 per new seller, beyond the anticipated missing of targets in the first year. Slashing onboarding time and cost made them more profitable faster. Under their refined onboarding process, new sellers spent weeks in the field with top performers. During the first week, they made sales calls with the team's number-one seller. During week two, they shadowed another department's sales leader. And through the third week, they spent time with a number-two seller. They never took a single step inside a sales classroom. The leaders even delayed product training until the onboarding was complete. By heading straight into the field (virtual or in-person) with a crew of all-stars, they learned much about the marketplace, including winning tactics. The new structure dramatically reduced ramp-up time while improving confidence, instilling strong skills, and providing hands-on experience with the company's products. Going the opposite route—**keeping people away from customers during onboarding—is among the worst things** you can do for a salesperson looking to get up to speed. Make coaching as effective as possible: put your sellers in the game—and in front of customers—as quickly as possible.

Guided Selling

Guided selling, or "just-in-time coaching," describes an advanced strategy becoming popular among my clients. Here, coaches serve up small bites of training and coaching aligned with CRM data and opportunities in specific phases. Picture a seller in the qualification phase of an opportunity worth $100,000. The CFO confirms the seller is competing against three companies. Using this data, CRMs, and other technology platforms like Allego—a sales coaching program—pull from a library a set of custom coaching and training snippets relevant to this particular opportunity. To expand the value of this technique, some companies also include feedback from reps, video messages, and implementation results. Upon closing a big win or suffering a significant loss, the seller records a short video (of between two and five minutes) discussing what went right or wrong. Uploaded to their system, this becomes part of a growing library of knowledge to enhance learning.

With guided selling, sellers can easily search for "just-in-time" suggestions around each unique selling scenario; rules within the CRM automatically serve up relevant content. Talk about converting your CRM into a sales enablement tool! Best of all, sellers love it. You gain an extraordinary return on investment without overly taxing anyone's time.

Nothing proves more powerful than getting coaching on a specific opportunity in real time. Never have I met a seller who wouldn't celebrate that level of feedback and support—practically an onboard compass identifying the right way to go. In fact, as I trained a group of financial product sellers, one asked, "Can I just take you with me? Can you hang over my shoulder?" With thanks for the compliment, I politely declined and shared that with just-in-time coaching tools, you achieve much the same effect: you bring up situation-specific scenarios and advice on your phone before heading into a meeting or jumping on an important call.

Getting Right on the Money: Quick Tip

Are you a solo entrepreneur? A seller working for a manager who won't coach? Do you even report to a manager? In some situations you must coach yourself. Carefully analyze your results for opportunities to improve. Develop a cadence to review such insights. Once a week—either early Monday or late Friday is ideal—sit down for half an hour and ask: *Where am I relative to goals for this week?* Determine plans for next week to either fill any gap or to continue leveraging your success. In your results to date and your pipeline, is enough there to hit your targets? If not, how might you ramp up prospecting? If there is, keep prospecting at the same levels and work on closing those deals.

Once a month do a deeper dive. Determine again whether you're ahead or behind, and reassess calculations based on such results. If you're behind, build that into your current target and prospecting efforts; if you're ahead, either change your calculations or keep them and hope to beat your target.

This methodical process helps keep your monthly targets on track and reduces the risk of small, neglected problems growing into big ones. For instance, if your goal is three new opportunities in a week, falling behind by one week may be little problem; after two or three weeks, though, you may be looking uphill.

Each quarter repeat the process with an even deeper analysis that takes about an hour to complete. Examine the gap between where you are and where you should be. Is your pipeline big enough to fill this gap? Do you need to prospect more? Do you need to close more? Do you need any help? Be your own source of growth and development—self-coaching can get you there.

Tools of the Trade

You cannot coach yourself or others solely by following your gut. As we've discussed, you must stay objective and disciplined. You must ferret out relevant data from your CRM (or a suitable substitute) to help you manage pipelines, gaps, opportunity creation, and results. Coach based on what you *know* to be happening, not on what you *feel* is happening. Using tools to your advantage ensures you possess everything you need to coach yourself or others effectively.

Allow me to share a dirty secret: most salespeople still underuse their CRM. At best they see it as bothersome; at worst they slam it as managerial overreach in the form of surveillance. Each time I coach a seller who regularly struggles to meet sales targets, I ask first about their CRM habits. Without fail I learn they underuse their CRM, if they use it at all. It sounds so basic I feel almost embarrassed to have to write about it, and yet I see it daily inside sales teams—so clearly, we need some straight talk.

CRMs exist because they work. All top sellers know this. A recent study by Innoppl Technologies found that 65 percent of sales reps who regularly use their CRM reach sales quotas. Compare this to the staggering 78 percent of those who avoid CRM falling short of their targets.

Just as troublesome is the common misperception CRMs serve only as "activity monitors." That same Innoppl study found 87 percent of sellers suspect managers adopt CRMs to police sellers' activities. This fear leads them to just "check boxes" in the system rather than take advantage of its true value.

Let's get real: CRMs help salespeople sell more by organizing work and highlighting connections they would otherwise miss among data fed into the system. Put another way, CRMs help manage and make sense of your data. When you or your team fail to update the system in a thorough and timely fashion, you sow bitter seeds of misfortune.

Mark, the CEO of Alexis, struggled mightily with both the quality and quantity of data in his CRM. After investing heavily in a new system, he struggled to get his team to enter information. As a result, he lost the ability to effectively coach and saw minimal return on his investment. Without data he gained no window on happenings within his market. His team offered the usual excuses:

"It's too much work."

"I keep all this in my own files."

"It doesn't work remotely."

"You're just asking so you can monitor me closely."

To overcome these objections, Mark and I staged an intervention of sorts. We hatched a plan: we would first force compliance, but we knew this would eventually lead to commitment. During a regular Friday sales meeting, Mark said: "From now on, every Friday afternoon you're going to come to the office and update your CRM. And you're staying until it's done."

The following Friday was a nightmare. Many stayed late. Some couldn't remember passwords. Others struggled to decipher their own handwritten notes. A few fell short in remembering what they'd done on Monday! Some grew frustrated and angry to find themselves in gridlocked traffic after they left. And yet, in week two they stumbled into an epiphany: by staying on top of updating their CRM on the fly, they could finish on time every Friday—and what's more, the process became even faster, because the information was fresh in their mind.

Getting serious about updating the CRM paid off for Mark and his people. They eliminated duplicate work by reducing physical note-taking and stepped away from the burden of inputting a boatload of data at once. Best of all Mark found the right data at his fingertips in real time, which in turn allowed him to make well-informed decisions in less time.

Create Success on Purpose

In sales it means little to know you're good at selling and closing; it matters that you know *why* you're good. If you can't determine the secrets behind your top performers' success, you miss out on their most important contribution; evidence represents a vital tool. Be deliberate about understating success in sales. As a coach your job is to help sellers operate in a conscious manner so they can reproduce success and leverage improved performance by teaching others.

Coaching Top Performers

We can now all agree top performers can help others elevate their success. But how do you coach top performers? If they already exceed targets with no signs of slowing down, should you even bother trying?

I've worked with many executives who find themselves on the fence about whether to coach star players. Their concern is always the same: "I don't want to meddle in their success and risk them thinking I'm a nag. If I try to tell them what to do, they'll get mad and leave!"

My response is this: stop treating top performers with kid gloves. Not the divas you make them out to be, they need and want coaching even more than your bottom performers. Use their ego, competitive spirit, and desire to win to your advantage.

Your top performers *absolutely must* be coached, regardless of how impressive you regard their numbers or how long they've exceeded expectations. **These sellers provide you with the best opportunity to advance your revenue,** so steer clear of the trap of implementing a "hands-off" policy. If you do, you do everyone in your organization a major disservice.

Getting Right on the Money: Quick Tip

What's the best way to coach top performers?

- **Let them drive.** Ensure they come to sessions with any requests they have of you and let them take the lead.
- **Let them talk.** Assign tasks that encourage your stars to speak about best practices for the organization. If you treat them like the leaders they are, they feel engaged and not only continue current behaviors but also put in the effort to continue to grow and excel. Remember: positive work ethic and practices are contagious. Other sellers are sure to catch the bug and get busy doing their own best work.
- **Keep sessions short.** Use these sellers' impatient nature to your advantage. For most top sellers, a thirty-minute session is best. Find a solution and let them go out and implement it right away.
- **Have them dissect wins.** Top performers love sharing their wins. By having them articulate exactly what they did to land the business, you make their process conscious, ensuring they can replicate it on purpose again and again.

- **Don't push it!** The last thing you want is to expose everything wrong with a particular seller in an attempt to improve them. This is a sure-fire way to send high-level talent to another company. Instead ask what they're doing well and how they could improve. Even the best producers often immediately identify their own weaknesses. Remember, let them be hands-on and lead the way in their own training.

Managers often feel wary of coaching their best. This is a big mistake. Think back to those overcoached athletes I mentioned. Not only do they receive extraordinary support, they also continue to train, learn, and grow. LeBron James and Steph Curry still show up at every practice, ready to work on skills and to seek feedback from coaches. This phenomenon extends well beyond athletics. Just check out who business coach Marshall Goldsmith lists as clients on his website, marshallgoldsmith.com, and you may discover that your favorite business moguls count on coaches behind the scenes to help them evolve. Coaching also keeps top performers from stagnating. The challenges you provide help them stay motivated. While you should always appreciate your stars for their hard work, you should also encourage them to learn more, do more, and sell more. Keep them engaged through consistent coaching. When they improve further and create even greater sales, they'll thank you for pushing them in the right direction.

Your Coaching Culture

Sales leaders hold an unwavering belief in their ability to deliver value to clients. They know the keys to success are transferable, because they have field-tested each themselves. People look up to leaders because they, too, want to carry a belief system of their own. When you communicate exactly how sellers can achieve value in their selling process—and you match such claims with results—they sit up and pay attention. A strong belief system improves your influence and your negotiation skills and, just as important, helps you identify who buys into your beliefs and who doesn't. Knowing this helps shape the coaching plan for each member of your team.

Okay. You've been handed your whistle and your cap. You're ready to build and grow a coaching culture, turning benchwarmers into next season's winners and helping "A" players reach even greater heights. By following the various actionable steps outlined in this book, you form a new mindset about selling in a marketplace that has changed fundamentally over the last decade.

This takes us to our final step together. Let's review all key points so you own a solid understanding of what you must do to capitalize fully on this changed landscape and stay Right on the Money.

SUMMING UP: MASTERING WHAT YOU CAN CONTROL

I wrote this book to better equip salespeople, sales leaders, and executives to respond to three massive and unprecedented trends reshaping today's marketplace:

1. An ***unprecedented shift*** in the sales landscape that moved the buyer into the driver's seat for both B2B and B2C transactions—an altogether new and game-changing development.

2. Deep ***denial*** persisting among many about how such shifts had already upended the traditional "rules" of sales and the purpose and role of salespeople—even before the global pandemic knocked everyone sideways.

3. A disturbing sense of ***helplessness*** among many, along with a profound longing for anything approaching ***certainty*** in a permanently changed and distressingly fluid landscape.

Knowing how to adapt one's outlook and habits in recognition of such sea changes in the marketplace renders one Right on the Money. As my friends Richard Citrin and Alan Weiss, authors of *Strategy-Driven Leadership* and *The Resilience Advantage*, respectively, remind us: the wisest response to today's adversity is to refrain from trying to define what the new "normal" looks like. Instead, approach things with *bounded optimism* and focus only on those factors within your immediate control.

Knowing your customer calls all the shots in this brave new world, you must balance customer centricity and Sales Velocity as much more than a mere sales strategy—you must permanently weave a Right on the Money approach into your organization's DNA. Everyone from your receptionist to your delivery drivers to your CEO must play a role in the sales process; every player must understand and listen intently to the customer's voice.

Make All Things Easier for Your Customer

My most successful clients regard it as part of their mission to make it as easy as possible for customers to buy from them. They are transitioning to online ordering and are revisiting all processes to accommodate buyers' demands for convenience and speed. They empower all employees to think of themselves as profit centers that can either attract or repel customers; in fact, such expectations are woven into measures of employee performance. These companies make sure the organization and its products are easy to find, to talk to, and to engage with. They meet their customers where these people and organizations hang out, and they devote themselves to sharing high-value insights.

How customer-centric are you and your organization? Review the early chapters of the book and, on a scale of one to ten, rate how well you meet the expectations of an evolving marketplace. We make it easier by providing a sample at www.rotm. me. For those aspects you rate yourself highly in, consider how to preserve this position of strength and decide how often you'll re-evaluate; for those on which you score poorly, prioritize areas offering the greatest opportunity to improve and start making tangible changes now.

Think Bigger about Your Company

The changing business landscape affects much more than sales. Its impact is felt throughout your organization. As such, any failure to generate the kind of revenue you desire may mean the rot goes deeper than the sales team; it may point to systemic weaknesses in other departments as well. Are marketing messages answering questions customers may be inclined to ask? Are delivery logistics designed for the convenience of the customer or the delivery person? Consider the role of each department and of each employee and make sure you equip each with the tools needed to work in tandem to delight the customer.

Connect Everywhere with Everyone

Despite its radical transformation, selling has always been, and will always be, a *people* business. Sellers today must make a commitment to connect with more people, to have more and better conversations, and to draw more people from within your organization into the customer interaction. You must embrace the new reality that strangers affect your sales; by constantly chiming in, you turn those strangers into loyal friends.

Know What Changes in a Landscape Where the Customer Sees You First Now

With your buyer firmly in charge of the sales cycle, what they desire more than anything else is instant and total gratification. Not *too* high a bar, right? All businesses today, from the few remaining mom-and-pop shops and boutiques to giant multinational concerns, must borrow a page from Amazon's playbook and focus on giving the customer exactly what they want and to let them have it right now. When you succeed the customer rewards you with quick sales, repeat orders, and, ultimately, evangelism.

Know How to Measure What Matters to Your Business

To ensure you're continually raising the bar, examine your Sales Velocity in real time and use it to spot trends. Track it by person and by team, and make sure every person understands how they can contribute to growth and greater success. What's more, keep exploring ways to pursue incremental improvements to each metric over time. Remember to download the calculator at www.rotm.me.

Build and Grow Your Coaching Culture

Remember that all sellers—even your very best—need ongoing and well-conceived support. The best sales managers do nothing but coach for at least 50 percent of their time. If they were once top sellers, they give up both the glory and their accounts and focus instead on achieving even greater glory by helping others excel. They never grow complacent or comfortable; they hold sellers to high but realistic standards and devote themselves to seeing each person on the team burst across the finish line (or they cut them loose).

In reading this book, you joined me on an epic, unpredictable, and at times unsettling adventure. We bid farewell to many moldy '70s-era habits that, over time, deteriorated from best practices to gremlins scuttling efforts to enhance sales. We toured today's radically transformed business landscape, exploring its maddening challenges and limitless opportunities. We discussed many ways you, as a seller and leader, can not only adapt—since you have no other choice—but also capitalize on huge changes.

Acquired knowledge never applied is useless, so you must commit yourself to put these strategies to work. Regain certainty in an uncertain world. Gain mastery over what's within your control. Be wise about data and grasp the differences between information and insight. When you adapt to all the "new rules" in this changed landscape—with your new road map in hand thanks to this book—you are **Right on the Money**. You possess the skills, policies, and practices necessary for sustained success; you're equipped to set the standard for the next generation of buyers and sellers.

You *can* do it. You *must*.

I'm grateful to you for including me on this journey, and I wish you the very best as you continue your own adventure. The road may be bumpy at times, but the future most certainly looks bright.

YOUR NEXT STEP. FREE ADDITIONAL RESOURCES:

I t was impossible to include everything in this book and keep it a manageable size. So, I've created a place for you to download resources that will help you implement the changes we discuss in the book.

At www.rotm.me you will find resources including (but are not limited to):

- video interviews with my clients on how they are implementing key Right on the Money concepts;
- templates and calculators;
- additional questions and examples; and
- coaching templates.

I will continue to add to these resources so check back often, stay in touch and reach out with questions and suggestions.

ABOUT THE AUTHOR

C olleen works with sales leaders to synergize the sales DNA of the organization to seize market opportunities. Whether designing strategy to target a new market or working with a team to improve its productivity, Colleen's results have attracted clients such as John Deere, Chevron, The Mosaic Company, Merck, Abbott, Merrill Lynch, Royal Bank, Dow, Adecco, Trend Micro, NCR and hundreds of other global organizations.

Time and time again, clients who work with Colleen note her frank, no-nonsense approach to accelerate sales while reducing effort and increasing profits. Colleen's practical strategies deliver immediate and lasting results.

Colleen is an award-winning consultant, bestselling author, and a Speaking Hall of Fame inductee. She is recognized as one of the foremost thought leaders on the future of selling by leading publications worldwide including being named the #1 Sales Influencer to follow by LinkedIn.

Colleen lives in Ottawa Canada with her husband Chris and her trusty writing partner, the Rhodesian Ridgeback Lady Llewyn. Like many sane Northerners, they escape the snow each winter to spend time in Florida.

Colleen's other books include *Honesty Sells* (with Steven Gaffney) and *Nonstop Sales Boom*.

A free ebook edition is available with the purchase of this book.

To claim your free ebook edition:

1. Visit MorganJamesBOGO.com
2. Sign your name CLEARLY in the space
3. Complete the form and submit a photo of the entire copyright page
4. You or your friend can download the ebook to your preferred device

Print & Digital Together Forever.

Snap a photo

Free ebook

Read anywhere